HAPPILY
IMPERFECT

STACEY SOLOMON

HAPPILY IMPERFECT

Living Life Your Own Way

Thorsons

Thorsons
An imprint of HarperCollins*Publishers*
1 London Bridge Street
London SE1 9GF

www.harpercollins.co.uk

First published by Thorsons 2019
This edition published 2020

1 3 5 7 9 10 8 6 4 2

© Stacey Solomon 2019

Stacey Solomon asserts the moral right to be
identified as the author of this work

A catalogue record of this book is
available from the British Library

ISBN 978-0-00-832289-2

Printed and bound in Great Britain by
CPI Group (UK) Ltd, Croydon

MIX
Paper from
responsible sources
FSC™ C007454

This book is produced from independently certified FSC™ paper to
ensure responsible forest management.

For more information visit: www.harpercollins.co.uk/green

Thank you to Joe and all of the incredible boys in our life.

Contents

HAPPILY IMPERFECT

INTRODUCTION:

Labels

Essex Girl: *A type of young woman, supposedly to be found in and around Essex, and variously characterized as unintelligent, promiscuous and materialistic.*

Oxford Living Dictionaries

Labels. We all have them, don't we? They're the reason I'm writing this book. I'm wildly, wonderfully imperfect, and my label as an Essex Girl proves it.

Am I an Essex Girl?

Absolutely!

Do I fit the stereotype?

Absolutely not! There's so much more to people than the labels we're given, and I want to share how I stay positive, how much I love my life, and how flawed yet happy I am, hence the title *Happily Imperfect*. This is how I am, and how I try to be, even when things feel less than ideal.

I'm far from perfect. I make mistakes, and that's okay – in fact, it's brilliant! This is the imperfect way I live my life:

I love my work and revel in my family and community. I want to share how I stay positive, and show you how I deal with life's ups and downs. I'll be giving you completely imperfect advice, telling you what helps me in the hope that it helps you too. Your life doesn't have to be perfect – far from it. You don't need to be, look or even act a certain way to be happy.

I'm going to celebrate all of my imperfections, and there are plenty of them! I'm a 'smother' (Smothering Mummy, as my boys call me), a buffoon of a girlfriend, a fairly idiotic daughter, and I'm incredibly lucky to be a telly personality too. It all goes to show that there's no right or wrong way to live wa-hoo!

Take from this book what you will. There is no single way to do things. I haven't been through major trauma: I just want to share my journey with you, so that you know the real me, the unfiltered me, the far-from-perfect me. I want to pull open the curtain of celebrity because the people on your screens are just that: people – exactly like you. They're no better or worse than anyone else. I'm passionate about breaking down barriers of all kinds – class, race, sexuality, whatever else holds people back or separates us. We're all human. Let's give ourselves a flippin' break from judging others and – most importantly – ourselves.

Let's go on annual leave from being told how to look, what to wear and who to be. Let's say thanks but no thanks to the advertisers and social media telling us how to do or be anything. We don't need to be thinner, richer, younger (!) or have a cut-glass accent. Those things don't make you special to others. You being the only 'you' is the single most important thing that makes you stand out from the crowd. What a boring time we'd be having if everyone was the same.

Sometimes labels overshadow our talents. I was lucky enough that that wasn't the case when I stepped onto the *X Factor* stage. I was last in the queue of thousands. I'd been waiting in an audition room packed with people until there was no one left except me, Zach and Mum. You can imagine what I looked like after spending sixteen hours in that space with my one-year-old. There was sick on my Converse trainers. My hair had been pulled every which way, and I wondered if I would ever actually get up there in front of the judges.

When they finally called my name, there was a rush of 'Oh, my gosh, this is really happening!' My heart was pounding and my mouth was as dry as if I'd eaten a bowl of sand. I felt my lips roll up like a blind – they literally curled up. I was *so* scared that the words of my song seemed to have vanished from my brain.

Standing there in front of the four people who would determine what happened next in my life, and the huge audience, I opened my mouth. Although the judges were surprised when they heard the girl from Dagenham's singing voice, the stereotypes didn't affect the opinions of Simon Cowell and the other panellists: Dannii Minogue, Louis Walsh and Cheryl Cole.

In the moment when all four gave me the thumbs-up, I realized I didn't need to be perfect: I just needed to be *me*.

Phew! I didn't have to waste my energy trying to be someone I'm not. Just then it was truly amazing to be me: Stacey Solomon, *X Factor* contestant, ex fish-and-chip-shop worker, single teenage mum. Just me.

By being totally myself, I hope I can encourage others to be themselves. The prejudice I've faced in my life has often pushed me in the direction I've needed to go. When I was labelled a single mum, when people tutted at me breastfeeding Zach on the bus aged eighteen, I used that feeling to drive me forward, to make a success of myself, pay my taxes and be a good mum.

When people said I'd never make anything of myself because I had a baby, I wanted to prove them wrong. I have a rebellious side, which was often seen as negative when I was growing up, but it worked in my favour. It can work in yours too. If you feel like you don't fit, like other people can't see how incredible you are, choose who you want to be, and prove them all wrong.

We don't have to be incredible, amazing or plain fabulous all the time. That would be draining. I try to look at the positive in each situation, and over time, I've found it the easiest way to be. I've discovered it's much easier to let go (most of the time!). Getting angry or frustrated uses energy I could be channelling into making life better.

Happiness has become my 'neutral' state. When I smile, act in a friendly or kind way, I feel I'm owning my state of mind, regardless of what somebody wants to say or do to me. I'm more in control of how I react. When I'm confronted with a tricky situation, I try to ask myself, 'Is it worth getting angry over this?' It almost never is. But, of course, there are times when I need to stand up for myself, and certain situations in which anger and grief are necessary. Life isn't always about smiling.

Every day I wake up alive and healthy, I feel I'm a winner. I feel privileged to be here on this amazing planet, but things don't always go to plan. Stuff happens. Life throws a curveball. That's when trying to see the glass as half full can help. It's helped me through a few challenging times.

Choosing to see the positive isn't always easy.

I find it extremely hard every time I go to Romford's Queen's Hospital children's ward, where my sister works, where I act silly to entertain the children. While I'm with them, I'm thinking those kids shouldn't have to be there: they should be outside playing, but life doesn't always go that way. And it often strikes me that many of the children are the happiest, most positive humans I've ever met. There are some things you cannot change, so I try to focus on the amazing work the doctors and nurses do, the love and dedication of the parents and the resilience of the children. I walk out more aware of how extremely lucky I am to have healthy boys. It brings real perspective to everything.

My book is all about affecting the things you can change, like your state of mind, but if you want to see the ultimate act of positivity, then visit people in hospital. They're the real heroes in action.

Life is imperfect. I am imperfect. We all are. I've learnt to love my quirks and idiosyncrasies, and those of my family and friends. Our faults can also be our biggest assets. My trusting nature means people take advantage of me sometimes, but it makes me kinder, and more open to others. Without it, some of the amazing folk I've met along the way might have passed me by.

I'm not going to tell anyone how to live or how to be happy, but I can share what works for me, as a flawed mum and partner, who occasionally shouts at her children in a usually messy home. Let's not drown in life hacks, personality hacks, parenting hacks – hacking ourselves to bits – because *that* stress is the worst. And let's remember to stop getting stressed about how stressed we are!

It's been a massive relief for me to accept that I probably won't ever have an Instagram-perfect home, face, body or partner. I probably won't make my family organic juices throughout the day, throw a fake reindeer skin over my spotless designer sofa or waft through my Moroccan-inspired garden in a silk kaftan. Just isn't happening.

Let's celebrate being capable of love, and embrace the imperfections all around us. Let's be kinder. What would the world look like if we were kinder to each other? It would be … almost perfect.

This book is about how my imperfections have helped me to live my best life. Thanks to them, I can make better choices about how to feel, what to focus on, and enjoy life.

I may be only twenty-nine, and I've broken a lot of rules, but I've learnt so much about love, being a mummy, and how to keep a smile on my face when the world seems bleak. Now I know what I need to do on my down days, when I've got Mum Guilt or I'm just sad, I want to share how I get through feeling hormonal, emotional or plain exhausted.

I've also decided to stop comparing myself with others or focusing on negatives. Halleluyah! I suffer from anxiety, so I've had to learn how not to worry about superficial things: it takes practice.

I want to bring you into my huge, crazy Jewish family. Today we would be labelled a 'broken family' but we didn't fall apart when Mum and Dad divorced.

Dad bought a house opposite us so my sister, my brother and I could live half the time at Mum's and half the time at his. Then he remarried and we grew into a blended family. It wasn't conventional but it worked. That was where I came from – and that's me.

This is an easy, no-stress book that celebrates all our weirdness and incredible-ness, with a few tips and bits of advice at the end of each chapter. I hope by sharing the things I've learnt along the way, I can help make life a little easier for you too. This is what makes me happily imperfect. Enjoy!

STAY POSITIVE

Labels! Everyone knows the stereotype of an Essex Girl – too much make-up, bleached hair, teetering on sky-high heels. She definitely lacks brains. Such a cliché! I could've let it hold me back, but I treasure my roots.

My accent is my member's card to my life. All my friends and family speak like me. Fundamentally, we're all good people with huge hearts, and that's what matters. My accent makes me approachable, and I've started to enjoy my label. I've embraced the so-called 'flaws' of my accent and working-class roots. Italia Conti might not have wanted me, but *The X Factor* did, and the way I spoke became an advantage: it made me stand out from the rest, and gave me the 'wow' factor when I opened my mouth to sing. I'll never forget the looks on the judges' faces. It was the moment my hopes and dreams crystallized, the start of everything. Thank goodness I'm an Essex Girl. Would Simon, Louis, Dannii and Cheryl have noticed me if I wasn't?

Look at the labels society may have stuck on you. Do they fit? Do they work for you? Do they define you? Can you own it or them, and make a positive from a negative? I've learnt that there's more scope to impress people when their expectations are low, so set out to surprise them. Take advantage of those expectations and have a bit of fun with them, just like I did. Make peace with your labels – they could end up serving you rather than defining you.

Use this book to look at what might be going on with you, and identify it as a stereotype, a cliché or a label. It can be as easily shrugged off as embraced. You are you, your utterly unique and amazing self, and that is more than enough.

CHAPTER 1

Letter to Me
(aged fourteen)

Dear Stacey,

Seriously, this isn't wierd at all.
I just want to say 'Hi' from the
future — and let you know that
things are going to be okay. I know
that right now you're stressing over
whether Bradley Watson will snog
you or that girl from the year above
at the party on Saturday, or
whether the spot that's threatening to
break out on your chin is going
to swerve the party or appear at
around 7pm on Saturday evening.
It all feels so important right now,
and you're probably really anxious,
but you know what? Life is going
to be totally imperfect and totally
brilliant.

I'm writing to you from the grand old age of twenty-nine (cue weird sci-fi music) to make sure you hang in there because your teenage years, well, to be honest, they're a bit dodgy. You're going off the rails. You're skipping school, hanging out at random tube stations smoking cigarettes and feeling bored. You're not even bothering to hide your skiving from mum! Seriously, if you want to get away with missing class, at least change out of your ever-so-attractive kappa tracksuit bottoms and hoodie before you go home. You could also try not leaving notes saying 'Let's go and have a ciggie behind the bike sheds,' in your blazer.

Message from the universe: Your mother goes through your pockets!

So when you're done with bunking off, drinking cheap alchopops with your mates and hanging out at Hornchurch station (seriously, Stace, why?), you need to get your s**t together because some big stuff is coming, and it's right around the corner.

If I told you you're going to be a broke, teenage single mum to a little boy, and that you'll keep turning up at X Factor auditions and being turned away, you'd probably think I was joking. I'm not. This really is your future, so keep believing in yourself and keep optimistic about everything!

Keep your dreams alive, because they'll pull you through some pretty dark times.

I know you're a happy-go-lucky fourteen-year-old, and you think you know best. We all do at your age. But, Stacey, you need to grow up- and fast - because your big break is coming, your stars will align, and you'll make it. Keep loving your son (yes son!) and know that, whatever anyone says, you're worth so much, and you're loved.

There's some other stuff I want to tell you. Maybe not as prophetic, but pretty darn useful anyway, such as:

* Boobs don't define you! (they're not as big a deal as you think.)

* Boys are unfathomable until you realise they're human, just like you.

* Your mates are your greatest consolation in life. You won't still be hanging around the bike sheds waiting for Bradley to leave school so you can 'randomly' bump into him, forcing him to walk home with you. Boys and, later, Men come and go but your friends are often there for life.

* Stop twatting around in class. You think you're being hillarious but in fact you're making a total arse of yourself and scaring the quiet kids.

* Refusing to stop eating pickled onion Monster Munch in class so that you have to stand through the entire lesson is not a good idea. Neither is skipping class to sit on the girls' loos (again, Stacey, why?). Both will earn you a spell living with Granny, & things get way stricter at Jewish school.

Your voice really will take you to places you never dreamed possible, so keep dreaming, keep singing. It'll all work out, I promise...

CHAPTER 2

The Big A

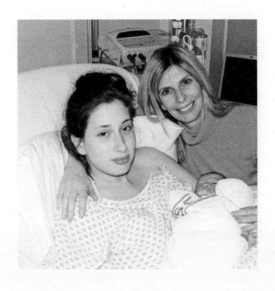

It started with prickles of sweat on my hands, then something like an electric current turbo-charged up my arms as I clutched my stuffed cat, Tootsie, and listened to the last words of our bedtime story. My older sister Jemma, who was eight, my brother Matthew, four, and I shared a bedroom. I was only six and, out of nowhere, I was terrified. It was a feeling I'd never had before. Because I was so young I didn't even have words for what I was experiencing but I recognized fear. My body started to shake. My mind started to whirr. I couldn't swallow. My breathing felt weird, like I had to think about it instead of just doing it. What was going on? I had to force each breath in, and each one out. I was starting to pant.

'Stacey, are you okay?' Mum peered into my bunk as she closed the book and started up towards the light switch.

'Don't leave me! Please don't go!' I begged, holding Tootsie even tighter. 'If I go to sleep I might die. I might never wake up again!'

I don't know where those thoughts came from, I just blurted them out.

Mum looked at me strangely. 'What are you on about, Stace? Of course you'll wake up again! You silly girl, you're just overtired. What you need is a good sleep, young lady.'

'No, Mummy. I'm scared.' I must have sounded so pitiful!

At that moment Dad stepped into the bedroom. 'It's time for sleep, Stacey,' he said firmly. 'Come on, let's leave them and let them get some rest,' he said, looking pointedly at Mum. Dad was strict about bedtimes, which now I understand. Back then I would never have dared challenge him, so I stayed in my bed, though each second was agony.

'There's nothing to worry about, Stacey, I promise you. We're here and you're safe. Now go to sleep,' Mum whispered, leaning over to kiss my forehead.

Usually she was able to soothe me but not that night. I stared after her as she tiptoed out. I didn't dare to move, sitting bolt upright in my bed, as Matthew and Jemma snored softly in their bunks close by. Our giant teddy, Sylvester – we called him Sylvia after one of Mum's friends, thinking it hilariously funny – was beside me. I cuddled up to him, dread filling me right up.

Every night Jemma and Matthew fell asleep before Mum had finished reading, but it usually took me longer to drop off.

'You've got a busy head, that's what it is, clever girl,' Mum would say, ruffling my hair proudly. I didn't feel clever. I just couldn't switch off my head like my siblings did at bedtime, and I wished I could! Mine was always sparking with thoughts and questions.

I don't know why I suddenly developed such a terror of going to sleep and dying. What could have triggered it? No flippin' idea. I was confused as much as scared, and I really believed in that moment that I'd drown in the blackness of sleep, never to wake up. Dramatic but true. The thought makes me shudder, even today.

'Don't go! I'll die if you go!' I whispered, but the door was shut, the room turned black, and I sat there, wanting to scream but instead panting, my eyes as wide as a rabbit's in the headlights. My breathing was becoming shallower and faster. *I'm going to die … I'm going to die …* My head was thumping. My body felt numb as I tried to draw air into my lungs. *What if I fall asleep and it's black for ever?*

The numbness spread from my feet into my legs and passed through my small frame. I felt heavy and even more frightened. I couldn't cry. I couldn't move. For what seemed like an hour, I sat there, my heart pounding.

Eventually – perhaps only a minute or so later – the feelings began to subside. I lay down, feeling really sick, my eyes eventually closing, but sleep stayed away.

That was my first panic attack and it was the start of my lifelong relationship with anxiety, or the Big A, as I call it. It was frightening because I hadn't a clue what was happening to me. From then on, I dreaded bedtime because I was scared it would come back, and it often did. I wanted to pretend it hadn't happened, and go back to being the happy child I was before it struck.

It's taken me a long time to make peace with my anxiety, to understand that it's a natural survival instinct, though I'd be lying if I said I'm totally comfortable with it.

I still experience panic attacks, though they're less frequent, and at least I now understand what is going on. I can also be open about my anxiety, which means I can share my experiences and, hopefully, help you guys. Worry isn't a taboo subject for me. I think the more honest we can be about anxiety attacks, the more we can all feel we're not alone, that we can talk about it and therefore help others who might feel isolated.

Anxiety creeps up on me when I hear about the death of a friend's friend or see something tragic on the news. Death is the only thing I'm properly scared of, whether mine or a loved one's. It freaks me out. In fact, I envy people who worry about their relationship ending, or their children moving far away because that stuff just doesn't bother me. I don't worry about whether I'll lose my job one day, or even if my boyfriend Joe and I will split up. I don't want any of those things to happen, but they aren't life-or-death. Dying is the only thing that is!

If I'm alive I can do anything, but I'm aware that death could touch me at any moment. None of us knows when our time is up. I don't want my life to end. I love my family, my children, my friends, and even Joe (sorry, babe, I couldn't resist saying that!). Every morning I wake up happy to be alive and grateful for all the amazing things that have come my way. The thought of being dead fills me with horror. I don't want to lose any of my loved ones and I don't want my life to end. It's as simple as that.

I know people will probably laugh at me for being so morbid when I'm only twenty-nine, but I grew up around Jewish grandmothers. If you want to learn how to worry about anything and everything, get a Jewish granny! Seriously, my nana (my dad's mum) would constantly say things like: 'Ugh! Don't go outside – it's cold!' or 'Ugh, if you don't eat breakfast, you'll starve!' or 'Ugh, you need a coat on [when it's twenty degrees outside]!'

Nana lived like everything was dangerous and she was permanently on the edge of a cliff. I wonder if it was because Dad's father died when he was young and she had young children to bring up on her own. She did an amazing job, but her anxiety definitely had an effect on me, though as a single mum I totally get where she was coming from.

When I look at my boys, Zachary, ten, and Leighton, six, I feel it's all down to me to look after them. I mean, who would have them if I died? Who would support them and guide them? I'm really lucky. I have a *big* Jewish family so they wouldn't be left on the streets. It's more like, who would love them the way I do? And there's no answer to that.

I grew out of the childhood panic attacks and spent my teenage years in an almost exactly opposite state: I felt indestructible. I'd spent ten years worrying about dying in my sleep and was still alive so I trusted life again. I actually believed that nothing bad would ever happen to me, and behaved accordingly. I had found my outspoken, rebellious side and loved it! It drove my mum mental.

When I went into labour with Zachary, everything changed and anxiety reared its ugly head again. I had no idea what to expect when I found out I was pregnant at seventeen. It was a big shock, closely followed by worry about the birth. I asked other mothers what their labours were like, and no one told me the truth. It was like there was a secret conspiracy to stop me knowing how traumatic childbirth can be. Looking back, it's obvious they were trying not to frighten me, to protect me from the often grim reality, but it also meant I had no idea about the pain of contractions. I was in labour for seventy-two hours. I couldn't believe how much each contraction hurt.

Ten years ago people weren't talking about it so publicly and honestly. There was no social media, no 'Maybe I can go on Twitter and ask for help or read blogs.' I was told, 'It'll all be all right in the end,' but that didn't prepare me for having giant needles in my spine, clamps up my vagina, and yet another person looking at my nunny.

It was the first time I truly felt my mortality, triggering all those old, anxious feelings. Giving birth was so painful, alien and undignified that it shook me. I found it utterly traumatic (don't let me put anyone off – I had a second child so it can't have been that bad, right?) and at one point I really thought I was going to die.

I realized I wasn't super-human. I'm not indestructible: I am, in fact, mortal. Perhaps I should've grasped that earlier in life. I'm a bit of a control freak. I like being on top of things. Anything I can't control sets off my worries big-time, and those feelings continue today.

Now I can't wait to have another baby. I go online, look up childbirth blogs, and birth stories, then work out all the options.

Anxiety is the bottom line for me. It sits under everything I do or am as a person. It comes on early in the day, a kind of itchy, troublesome restlessness that creeps over me, making everything I do seem strange and forced. It's usually when a friend rings and says, 'Did you know so-and-so got diagnosed with cancer?' or 'So-and-so died yesterday of a brain haemorrhage,' and it stays with me all day. It's the understanding of how fragile life is. It's much later, when I get into bed, when the kids are asleep, when my filming is done for the day, and there's nothing to distract me, that I go into a full-blown panic attack.

If I try to relax that only makes things worse. My breathing becomes something I have to think about, just like when I was a child, and that's when I know I'm having an attack. My body feels numb, heavy and paralysed. I have pins and needles in my hands. I can't swallow, and feel like I'm going to faint. I'm like that for about two minutes but it feels like for ever.

So, what do I do? I've come to terms with the fact I cannot stop the attacks when they start. I have learnt that the only way through is to accept it. I can't change who I am so I accept that I'm someone who has panic attacks. It's part of me, just like the colour of my eyes or the way I speak.

Rather than try to stop one, I concentrate on each moment, focusing on what is happening rather than trying to deny it. It sounds counterintuitive but, slowly, I was less freaked-out when I had one. Over time each attack felt less severe. I had to see an attack for what it was: a response to unhappy news that left me feeling powerless. A panic attack began to seem a logical response to whatever had happened. Once I understood the cause, I was able to sit through each one, and understand it. In doing so, I lost some of my fear of the actual attacks.

Afterwards, I can't sleep, so I'll clean the house, at 1 a.m., if need be, and eventually I might get a few hours' sleep. These days the attacks are fewer. I don't know why. I tried every technique I could, including cognitive behavioural therapy (CBT), yoga, Rapid Eye Movement Therapy (EMDR – Eye Movement Desensitizing and Reprocessing Therapy) and hypnotherapy. They all helped in small ways, and may be useful to anyone experiencing panic attacks. Do seek help and try different techniques if you suffer from anxiety – it really is worth it. In the end, though, it was accepting my anxiety, and enjoying my life despite the attacks, that made the difference for me.

I have learnt that if I allow each attack to happen without trying to stop it, it will work its way out. When I'm in that scary place, when my body is freaking out and my mind is telling me I'm going to die any second and leave my babies bereft, it feels like it'll never end. That's why I talk about it to friends and family. Somehow the act of talking, of being open about it, makes it seem less overwhelming.

If anxiety is part of you too, you'll know that feeling – the first few prickles of sweat, the nagging thoughts, the sensation in the pit of your stomach that tells you an attack is under way. You may feel light-headed, restless, have racing thoughts, faster breathing, and your heart is beating, it seems, at a thousand miles an hour.

At times like that it's impossible to see the bigger picture, to know that this excruciating feeling will last for a few minutes at most. Knowing your triggers and building a support network of friends, family and GP are invaluable in dealing with anxiety.

My trigger is always health-related. I know that the Big A will creep up on me and take me hostage at night if something upsets me.

I've learnt to differentiate between nerves and full-blown anxiety. For example, I get nervous before I go on *Loose Women* or before I sing. That it isn't anxiety because during an attack I feel like I'm going to die. I can't control that at all. I've been with *Loose Women* for years but I get a bit nervous still because I care so much about my job. I want to do well. That isn't the same as an attack. Before a show I can calm my nerves by telling myself that no one wants me to fail, the girls have got my back, or I remind myself that I'm capable of doing my job: that's why I was hired. I can create a positive mindset through experiencing nerves.

Positive self-talk is empowering because it helps me to keep my nerves in check so I can use them to try to do a better job. I like feeling that I'm giving something my very best shot.

If I'm honest, I have days when I sit on the panel and feel under-qualified, or unsure of my opinion, but at those moments I make a conscious effort to tell myself I'm good enough, and that it's okay to be unsure or even to change my mind on an issue. I tell myself it's okay to be nervous. If I felt nothing, I would wonder whether I wanted or cared about my work.

Knowing my triggers, working with my body and mind, and letting go of the need to stop my anxiety has helped me to keep the attacks in perspective, even to celebrate them. I find that turning a big negative into a positive is the way forward, though it takes time and understanding to achieve. I see my GP regularly, and I make sure my family and I eat healthily and do loads of outdoor play. I focus on creating a happy, balanced home and work life. The Big A can be a positive, even if it often doesn't feel that way. The challenge for me is to remember that, and keep living my life the best way I know how.

STAY POSITIVE

Find someone neutral or trustworthy, perhaps a GP, family friend, partner, or mental health professional, and just open up. There's nothing to be ashamed of. Speaking up on any mental-health issue is brave and honest, and will make things easier.

You may need further professional help, which may include medication or talking therapies. Work at understanding your triggers.

Recognize that anxiety is part of you – and is no different from any other illness. If you break your leg, you go straight to a doctor, and it's the same with panic attacks. Treat your condition as an illness rather than as something to be ashamed of.

CHAPTER 3

Ugly Duckling

The pretty girls at school were petite with cute button noses, smooth, shiny hair, sculpted eyebrows, long lashes and fuzz-free skin.

Then there was me. I was gawky. Ridiculously tall, with frizzy, unmanageable hair – barely there eyebrows and lashes, and a thick Yeti-like fuzz of body hair.

How did I get through school with those 'gifts' from Mother Nature? I just didn't realize how unconventional I was until people pointed it out to me. Even then, I was blissfully unaware of what people classed as pretty or otherwise. I hadn't really thought about my looks until then. I'd concentrated on developing my personality. I could make people laugh, and if I was naughty and funny, I had friends. I thought less about what I looked like, and more about who I was.

You could say that was where it all began for me. I had to cultivate my character because my looks didn't mean anything to me. My Shallow Hal approach to life meant that looks were irrelevant to me. Whether someone was kind, funny or smart was way more important than how they looked. I still feel that today.

Saying that, I knew I wasn't cute on the first day I walked through the gates at high school with the rest of my year group, and someone, an older child, said quite loudly: 'Ugh, she's not little …' And by 'little' they meant cute or sweet, or even 'resembling someone my own age'.

I didn't resemble anyone of my age. I didn't fit my year group. My body didn't fit my age. I was much taller and awkward, with fully developed boobs yet I still had milk teeth. Go figure.

I basically had an adult's body, plus all the accompanying hormones, with a child's face and emotional development. I was a complete mismatch. As soon as I heard that first 'ugh', I knew I was going to have to work harder than the other girls to be liked. As a kid, I'd always longed to be the cute one, the little one, but I never was. I was always the gangly one with shocking hair and tufty eyebrows. It didn't take me long to realize that none of the boys my age fancied me. They all went for the smaller girls with the straight sleek hair and button noses.

My hair was long but it was frizzy, so much so that my sister Jemma and I nicknamed our hair the 'Jewish-fro', or Jew-fro for short. Straighteners hadn't been invented, and if they had, I wouldn't have been allowed to buy them. Neither my mum nor my dad was vain and they'd have laughed at me if I'd said I needed to buy something to straighten my hair, though they relented when I was older. They thought we were beautiful as we were – which until then I'd believed. School had set me straight. I like to describe my 'fro in those days as part Joan Rivers, part Cher, part Monica-from-*Friends*-when-she-goes-to-Barbados. A fright, basically.

By the time I hit year seven, I had braces to add to the mix. Another nail in the coffin of my physical appearance. My front teeth were so far apart I liked to joke they had had an argument and were trying to get away from each other. At one point, pre-brace, I could fit a pound coin in the gap. My eyebrows had become small tufts that sat waving at me from over my eyes, and I'd been blessed with thick black hair all over my body except in the places that girls want it. My body was, I thought, horrendous. I was embarrassed by it and by my face. I wanted to stop time so I could go back to being young, but my physique wasn't letting that happen.

When (shock! horror!) someone finally fancied me, it was a boy from year eleven (when I was still in year seven). I found that disgusting because, back then, I thought he was way too old for me. Practically ancient! Also, the girls in his year took his liking for me as treachery, and blanked me, which wasn't pleasant, especially as I never encouraged him.

All in all, I was pretty insecure. I knew I would never be the pretty one in class, so I felt I had to earn people's friendship by acting out and generally being as loud, naughty and funny as I could.

I had to make myself likeable – it was a survival mechanism, but it taught me so much. My dad had always been very sociable. If we went to Butlins on holiday, he'd always be the parent who made friends with everyone, who led games with the kids, or got up for the talent contest. I really admired how well he got on with everyone, and how much effort he put into meeting people and honing his social skills. When I was a child he would say to me, 'Go on, go out and make friends,' or 'Be confident. Go and join in.' He had the knack of bringing people together. I always wanted to be that person, and being the ugly one at school laid the foundation for it.

So, I told jokes, messed about and did stupid things to build my friendship group because there was nothing I could do to change my appearance. I felt I had to work way harder than the attractive girls to fit in and be accepted, and that people had to have a good reason to want to be friends with me. Rightly or wrongly, that had a huge impact on the development of my character.

I rapidly became the class clown and loved my friends, who came from across the spectrum of the year group, including the popular ones, the pretty ones and the clever ones. I was just friends with everyone. I made sure I was the one you could have a laugh with and was great fun to be around.

Louise was my hero. She was popular, pretty and naughty, so, to me, she was endlessly mysterious and fascinating. All the boys loved her, and I looked up to her. My mate Joelly was just like me, really silly and childish in her tastes and behaviour. We both found really uncool things funny, and shared a secret liking for a babyish cartoon called *The Land Before Time*. Neither of us would have admitted at school to liking it – it would've been social suicide – but together we'd laugh over our favourite bits.

I was so rubbish at lying that I always got caught out. When I went off to school, I'd take my skiving clothes in a plastic bag. Mum always left by 7 a.m. for work so I didn't have to worry too much about being caught then. But I'd get home, still dressed in my joggers, hoodie and trainers, to find Mum staring at me, asking why on earth I wasn't wearing my school uniform. D'oh.

Basically, I was questioning the system at the same time as not feeling aesthetically 'good enough'. I was working hard on every other part of me to compensate, and at times I definitely took it too far, but underneath it lay the strong belief, passed on to me by my amazing parents, that personality outweighs physical appearance. The thing I care most about, regardless of how I look, is who I am as a friend and a mummy, and I try to be as decent a person as I can possibly be.

The seed of self-esteem must have been planted in me by my parents because as I got older, and grew into my body, I grasped that my worth was as a complete human being, and didn't rely on looks or achievements. I became more confident as people liked me for who I was, and the more sure of myself I became, the more boys started fancying me. I realized there was so much more to me than looks. I was growing up.

My parents had always told me that beauty is subjective, that everyone found different things attractive: there was no fixed idea of beauty. They instilled in me a belief that beauty is a state of mind: if I felt attractive, I would be attractive. In a weird way, this started coming true. The more at ease I was with how I looked, the more people were attracted to me. It was a self-fulfilling prophecy.

It took me a long time to 'find' myself, and by that I mean accept and love myself. It didn't happen overnight. School was a bad time for me, and probably for most people. You don't know who you are. Your looks and your body are changing. There's a lot to go through when you're young and vulnerable. When I accepted those changes, I started letting go of any anxieties I had about who I was and what I looked like.

Zachary's arrival had a massive impact on me. Everything I'd ever worried about suddenly seemed superficial because I had brought life into the world and I was entirely responsible for him. Even though the birth was difficult, I entered into a Shallow Hal period of happiness with my body – I was totally oblivious to the shape, weight and look of it. Instead, I marvelled at how my boobs could feed a tiny human, how I'd created little fingers and toes, and a beating heart, a person in his own right. My body was brave and amazing. *Look what I can do!* I felt like saying to anyone who'd listen. *Look! I can make fingernails and kidneys and hair!*

I was convinced I'd snapped back into shape after his birth and carried on regardless, wearing tiny bikinis on holiday and squeezing into skinny jeans. Looking at photographs of myself in those days makes me laugh. I clearly hadn't snapped back at all. I carried extra baby weight for quite a while but I really didn't know, and even if I had, I wouldn't have cared a jot. I'd made a little boy. I was utterly impressed by myself.

After that, I refused to see my 'flaws' – the things I'm told by the media and advertisers that I should hate about my body. I realized I had to let go of what society was telling me. I was a perfect version of *myself*, and I felt beautiful. At last, I accepted that I could choose to feel those things, and that there was no perfect formula for attractiveness. We're all beautiful, regardless of what we're told we should look like. We can determine how attractive we feel. I get to decide whether I'm pretty or not and I refuse to give that power to anyone else.

I feel just as beautiful without my hair extensions, false eyelashes or fake tan. I feel amazing when I've got no make-up on and my hair is pulled back into a messy bun. Who is going to tell me otherwise?

I do all the make-up stuff, the glossy hair and fake lashes because it's fun. I love dressing up. I love being able to change my appearance according to my mood, and I have a laugh with it. I never feel I *need* to do all that just to be acceptable. Anyone following me on Instagram or Twitter knows I'm just as happy to post pictures of myself without make-up as I am when I'm glammed up.

Being with Joe has also made a huge difference. He thinks I'm stunning, full stop. He loves me and thinks I'm the prettiest girl in the world, and that helps me feel I am because it's how he sees me. There are many mornings when he wakes up and he has my false eyelashes stuck to his neck or back, and sees me with mascara streaked down my face and greasy hair. He doesn't care. He loves me just as I am.

I'm not saying we need to have a partner to validate our sense of being beautiful, but it elevates my confidence for sure. I have had times in relationships where I've felt insecure, and others have projected their insecurities onto me. I freed myself from those situations and soon understood that someone else's view of me didn't have to be mine. Joe is amazing at being the total opposite of that. I used to hide my insecurities by being loud and funny. I'm still pretty loud, and I love having a laugh, and making people smile, but I do it because that's me. I have nothing to hide any more – and that feels amazing.

I'm in control of how important, beautiful and intelligent I feel, and I stay vigilant: I notice when negative thoughts come into my mind, and talk positively to myself in response. We all have them, those creeping, gloomy 'I'm not good enough' thoughts. When they come in I bat them away. They still turn up every day, though far less than when I was younger.

If you've ever felt like an ugly duckling, like I did, then I'd advise you to take your head out of your phone for a second and look around you. I'm always surprised by the difference between real and online life. It's comforting to lift my head and see that everybody else out there is like me. Nobody has yet invented a real-life skin smoother or airbrushing tool, so outside our laptops and mobiles, there are no perfect-looking humans, or CGI characters. What a relief! Everybody is beautifully different, and it's those differences that make us *people*, rather than characters in a fantasy version of life. It makes them real.

The reality is that we don't notice people unless they're directly connected to our lives. We feel that everybody is looking at us all the time, but *are* we being looked at? Probably not. The narcissist in me, says, 'Oh, maybe I can't go out in my unicorn slippers with half my eyelashes hanging off', but why am I worrying what the world thinks I look like? Why do I genuinely believe that the world is so interested in what I look like when I'm doing the supermarket run? It's not! Take great comfort in the fact that nobody cares and that's a really good thing.

It is never good to judge ourselves on looks alone. Why would we do that to ourselves? I look at my body and think, I can make stuff with my hands, or My legs can run, walk or do silly dancing – and that's incredible!

I'm no ugly duckling – neither inside nor out.

STAY POSITIVE

When we're feeling less than radiantly beautiful, which, let's face it, can be a lot of the time, there's a little trick that helps. Look at yourself in the mirror and tell yourself that you love yourself, and that you're an awesomely amazing human being. It works. Try it for a week. Stand in front of a mirror every morning just before you leave home, and tell yourself you look amazing. It only takes a minute, and it feels super-weird at first, but the benefits are surprising. That minute of appreciation and self-love can help you face the world outside the front door. That confidence-inducing self-talk, celebrating your awesomely imperfect reflection, can be really powerful in helping you live your best day possible, while imparting a little Ready Brek glow of courage and inner beauty to help you on your way.

CHAPTER 4

My Tribe
(My Big Jewish Family)

Three words sum up my childhood: Friday. Night. Dinner.

It was always held at Nana's tiny two-bed Jewish flat in north London. It really was a Jewish flat because the block had been built after the war to help refugees settle in London. It was next to Manor House tube station, and every Friday after school we'd all pile into those small rooms. By 'all', I mean my mum and dad and us three siblings, then later my step-mum Karen and her children, my aunties Marilyn and Alison, their children, plus my dad's brother Sonny and his family. Ten kids at least, assorted adults and the biggest vat of homemade chicken soup you've ever seen.

Playing with my cousins was the highlight of each week. I don't know how we all managed to fit into the flat and play happily together yet we did.

'Stacey, stop mucking about and help your nana! Matthew, stop chasing Jemma and set a good example ...' My dad's voice would rise above the melee, but we largely ignored him and carried on playing, safe in our family universe.

'Bubbe, of course I'll help you. Would you like me to sing as I lay the table?' I'd shout above the din. 'Bubbe' is the traditional Jewish name for 'Grandmother'. We've never been massively Jewish – we celebrate the Sabbath each week, of course, and Hanukkah, but that's about it, these days. I wouldn't dream of denying my family access to Christmas, Easter, Diwali or any festival outside Judaism.

Nana's eyes would twinkle and she'd shrug in that wholly Jewish way, which was permission enough for me to belt out my favourite chart hit of the moment as she stirred soup and fried dumplings ready for the feast – it went on through the evening due to lack of space.

I had an ulterior motive. If I entertained the adults, made them laugh and sang songs to them, they gave me second or even third helpings. It was a totally primal instinct. If I acted like a performing seal, telling jokes, making everyone laugh, they'd throw me a fish! I really felt I was there for their pleasure, and what I got from it was more food and the feeling I could fit in with the adults.

The first serving of chicken soup with *kneidlach* had the kids crammed round Nana's cramped dining-table. Even a whiff of that distinctive smell takes me right back there, slurping the clear soup with its yellow stain from the chicken, the noodles, carrots and unbelievably tasty dumplings – if anyone left one I'd have it. The table was surrounded by random garden chairs, eight in total, though it only really fitted four.

Next, the adults would eat their soup so we'd all swap over, though I'd always go back for more delicious soup – Jewish penicillin, as Nana called it. Then we'd have the main course, a roast chicken with yellow rice. No matter how many times my dad or I have tried to make Nana's yellow rice, we have always failed to reproduce the warm spiced flavour. Most of the time we wouldn't have pudding because by then Nana was too exhausted from cooking, but if we were lucky, I mean *reeeally* lucky, she'd make us meringues. It's another family mystery as to how she got them so chewy on the inside and crunchy on the outside. I've never been able to master her recipe, and I don't think Dad's ever managed it either. Most of the time we got a fruit pop – a long stick of iced water and sugar – and were happy with that.

Nana died aged eighty-six. She never got to see either of my boys. Zachary was born a couple of years after she passed, which, even after all this time, still makes me feel sad. Those evenings were legendary. In fact, it was an epic childhood, though by many people's standards we had very little except each other. Nana never had a spare penny in her life, but if she had, she'd have given it to one of us children. She thought she had everything, though, because she was rich in family and love.

My family has given me a sense of belonging that has carried me through all the hardships and times when I thought I wouldn't make it. Their love and support have defined and shaped me. I'd be nothing without them. I know how lucky I am to have them. They are my tribe, my clan, my brethren.

Growing up, I never really appreciated how close we all were, and it's only since I've been a mum that I've realized how important family has been to me, and how I'd almost taken it for granted. For instance, Jemma and I used to fight loads. We argued so much that Dad built a fake wall out of plasterboard, which cut our shared room in half, including the window, to separate us. I was gutted because it meant that Jemma's clothes weren't so accessible for me to steal – that was what lots of our fights were about.

The other part of me was thrilled to have a space of my own even though it was hardly bigger than a cardboard box. It meant I could spend hours on the phone to my friends and Jemma wouldn't be able to snitch on me – another cause of our arguments. Despite that, as Jemma and I grew up we became the closest of sisters. I call her every day and now we're best friends.

Strong women run in my family. Nana, who was the daughter of Polish immigrants, brought up her four children single-handed and alone after my grandfather died when Dad was young. Nana Toby, as she called herself – she hated her real name 'Mathilda' – was progressive in her views. She let my dad build a darkroom in her cupboard when he became interested in photography, which later became his profession. Later, she looked after us three when Mum had to leave early in the morning for work. I was still at primary school before Mum and Dad divorced. Mum worked for the Department of Social Security while Dad was setting up his photography business, which meant that neither parent could be there in the mornings to get us ready for school.

When my mum left quietly for the office, so I wouldn't be upset, I always found her out, ran to a top window and cried, 'Don't go! Don't leave me!' I was never one for understatement.

I was eight years old when my parents sat us down one day and told us they were separating.

'Jemma, Stace, Matt, we've got something to tell you,' Dad began.

'Move over,' Jemma hissed at me, wiggling her bum into the space where I was trying to sit.

'No, you move. *Muuum*, Jemma's sitting on me!' I wailed.

All three of us were crammed into the tiniest, ugliest brown leather sofa you can possibly imagine.

'Listen, you three. This is important,' said Mum. 'We're going to divorce because me and your dad love each other but we're not *in love* any more.'

There was silence, broken by Jemma bursting into tears.

'Oh,' was all I managed to say. Jemma was very upset, and I assumed I should be too, but our parents made it so easy and friendly that I wasn't sad for long. Matthew took it hardest. He was only seven when they split up, so he found it really confusing.

I'd had no clue that Mum and Dad's relationship was ending. They were so amicable, though we always knew when Mum was having a little cry about it: she'd hoover downstairs and we knew not to disturb her.

I think Mum had been feeling neglected because Dad worked so hard setting up his photographic company, but the reasons for their separation were never discussed. I always felt it was their business, not ours. Dad moved out, and not long afterwards he bought the house in our road. Each week, Mum had us from Sunday to Wednesday, Dad would pick us up from school on Wednesday and we'd stay with him for the rest of the week. They made it so smooth. They did the most selfless thing by putting us first.

A few years later, in 2000, when I was at the end of primary school, Dad met Karen. He introduced us to her that summer. Instantly, we loved her and she loved us. All credit to my mum, she made a huge effort to be nice to Karen and they got on really well. If Mum hadn't liked her, we'd have struggled.

As an adult, I look back at that time and can see how difficult it must have been for Karen, fitting into a close family. She and her children, Aaron, Samantha and Ray, came on holiday to Turkey with us, and it must have been strange being there with all of us, including my mum, while she was starting a new relationship. Dad was so happy, and she was such a lovely lady, that the holiday didn't feel awkward at all. I'll never forget that Karen bought me a book for the plane, *The Prince of Egypt*. It was the first time our new extended family had had a holiday together. To me, it was exciting, different and lovely. Dad was happy. Karen was happy – and so were we.

Once Dad and Karen had moved in together, half of our week was spent with our bigger family. The first time my new step-siblings stayed overnight with us, I insisted my new sister Sam slept in my bunk with me. When it came to bedtime, we lay there silently for what seemed like ages. It was really awkward. I didn't know her or she me. All of a sudden Sam put her foot out and caught the white sheet, which made me exclaim that her foot looked like Julius Caesar because it was wrapped in a toga.

'It's Julius Cheeser!' one of us yelled, and then we were laughing. We laughed so loudly and for so long that Dad had to come and tell us to stop. After that, whenever we stayed over, there'd be silence, then one of us would shout, 'Julius Cheeser!' We still do it today –though we've given up sharing a bunk bed!

I don't know how Dad and Karen could afford to feed us. We'd walk in from school and all six of us would head straight to the fridge. Most of the time Dad cooked.

One evening we'd all sat down at the table. 'Oi, budge up, Stace,' Matt said, elbowing me in the ribs.

'Hey, watch it! I'm bigger than you,' I retorted, giving my little brother a mock-grimace.

'Yes, yes, Stace, you look terrifying.' Dad grinned. 'Now, everyone, sit still and let me put this down.' He was carrying a large baking dish, which he put in the centre of the table with a flourish. There was a brief moment of silence while we registered the food, then the babble started up again, with laughing, fighting, teasing and squabbling.

I looked around me, knowing my life was messy but utterly complete. My new step-mum, Karen, was laughing at one end of the table, while Dad served up huge portions of his homemade shepherd's pie. My sister Jemma, my polar opposite in character, was chatting to our stepsister Sam, while stepbrothers Aaron and Ray (and later half-brother Josh) mucked about with Matt. It was a glorious mish-mash of children and adults, our blended family in action.

'Arrgh, Dad! You've put loads of chilli in it again!' I shouted, feeling the sudden burn.

'It's meant to be shepherd's pie!' Matt gulped down a glass of water.

Dad beamed, as happy as anything with his latest creation, while we coughed and went bright red in the face. I'd never seen so much water drunk so quickly by a group of children! Other times, we'd be sweating from the heat of the spices he'd jazzed up our dinner with, and he'd never relent.

'If you don't eat it, there's nothing at all,' Dad would say, and I'm the same with my boys, except I don't lace everything with chilli. I leave that to my father.

Afterwards we bickered as usual over who would wash, dry or put away the dishes. No one ever wanted to dry them. The job everyone wanted was putting away and we fought fiercely over it.

My family has given me the strongest moral compass. They taught me always to try to do the right thing, and to know how important people are. They taught me to have compassion and empathy: you never know what someone is struggling with. They may seem grumpy but they could be going through a very bad patch. Living with so many family members taught me to have consideration for others, and patience, especially when they're enduring difficult emotions. When I complained about my sisters or brothers, one or other of my parents would say, 'Hang on, Stace, don't just think about yourself. Look at *why* they're acting the way they are.'

That message has stayed with me, and I'm so grateful to them for that perspective. My family showed me that we could stand together and help one another, even during a divorce, and that we can have so much fun together. Just having each other was enough.

This became the blueprint for my parenting. I hope I'm able to be a smidgen of the parent to my kids that my mum and dad, and stepmother Karen, were to me. I really hope that with my boys I can bring joy into the simple things, without lots of stuff, the way I was brought up.

I want the values that were instilled in me – kindness, consideration for others, tolerance for people around me, togetherness and love – to be passed down to my children. I work really hard to achieve that. I'm just so grateful for everything my family did for me, and everything they still do today.

I wouldn't be the person I am today without my family. I have a huge amount of respect and admiration for every-one in it. I can't imagine what it's like not to have a family unit as close and loving as mine. Meeting Karen made me realize that family doesn't have to be blood-related. Anyone we love can be a surrogate parent, sibling, aunt or uncle to us. Family can be anyone – friends, pets, partners: it doesn't have to be biological to be real.

My family set-up isn't perfect by any stretch of the imagination. My parents divorced, and we blended two families together. I have two children by different partners, and now I'm not with either of them. Yet, despite that, we have thrived and loved, and I feel so fortunate we have each other. Why do we worry about being a perfect family? There's no such thing, only the love we have for those closest to us.

My parents' behaviour was a huge influence on the way we dealt with the divorce. It was their positivity that made our lives carry on so smoothly. There are lots of circumstances in which it is impossible to have that kind of break-up – I've discovered that in my own relationship history. It is also worth noting that it is completely out of any child's hands as to how their parents deal with separation or divorce. It's wholly up to them, and many may be unable to move on without conflict or difficulty. We all try to do the best we can.

It's important to recognize also that the breakdown of relationships doesn't necessarily define our parenting. We can make mistakes, or find we can't deal with our exes as easily as perhaps we'd like. That doesn't mean we've failed. It just means that real life is challenging and complex – and family relationships most of all.

I believe that my children can become whoever they want to become, despite our immediate family circumstances. I have to strive to be the parent I want to be, providing a happy and steady home for my boys that is full of love. It's all I can do.

I try to stay positive and kind about all the people involved in raising my children, which, although it can be tough at times, it is of the utmost importance to me as being a single mum isn't easy. That would be my main piece of advice to anyone who is reassessing their tribe right now.

My family is my backbone. Every day I give thanks for each and every one of them.

STAY POSITIVE

My parents were united as parents, regardless of what was going on between them, and they always spoke about each other in a positive light, with love and respect. I try hard to do the same with my own children and their fathers. It isn't easy, none of this is, but when I look at how happy my boys are, I know it's worth the extra effort.

How can you be more positive in your family relationships? Are there relatives or partners you can deal with more gently, or be more understanding about their troubles or behaviour? Can you stop yourself reacting in a negative way, even just a little? Your tribe is just that, your group of other flawed people trying to do their best, often in ways that may not be comfortable for you. It's when I see this that I remember love is a verb, and I can choose to express it in my actions, even if that means biting my tongue.

CHAPTER 5

Recipes That Say Love
(Version 1)

G etting a word in edgeways around our dining-table at mealtimes, especially on Friday night, was impossible unless you learnt to shout, make people laugh or debate passionately. With six siblings, and relatives coming out of the floorboards, we still have supper together on every Sabbath because it's our tradition. I have at least fifteen people round my table.

Pretty much everything about my personality was formed round the dining-table. I learnt to talk really fast, like *really* fast, so I could get out what I needed to say before someone interrupted me. My head has always been filled with a million thoughts – and a million things to say. I guess my telly career thrives because of this so I'm very happy with this imperfection!

When you're one of seven children, you aren't heard if you don't talk loudly. I learnt how to debate, how to engage in adult conversation, and I learnt about love. It was served up each evening amid the noise and the elbowing, the jokes and the occasional tears. Now, food for me is a form of love, and I serve it up to my boys every evening. I spend a lot of my life cooking. I see it as my service to my family, and all of it, absolutely all of it, expresses the love I feel for them. Friday-night dinner is the heart of our week, and has been since I was a child.

All these recipes are filled to the brim with love – the love oozes from them – and I dish it up unapologetically. I tell my boys I love them a hundred times a day, and that's still not enough for me.

Nana's Chicken Soup and *Kneidlach*

Nana always had a pot of her Jewish penicillin bubbling on the stove. Nowadays it would be described as 'bone broth' and sold for six pounds a pop in trendy Shoreditch, but it has been the staple of our lives. The chicken is usually a broiler bought from a kosher butcher so it has no giblets, but you can use any old chicken, though I'm told organic is best. This soup is meant to simmer from 7 a.m. to 7 p.m. for the best flavour but two hours is fine!

Serves 4
You'll need:

For the chicken soup
1 x 1.5kg broiler chicken or any chicken will do
1 onion, peeled and roughly chopped
2 sticks of celery, roughly chopped
2 carrots, roughly chopped
1 chicken stock cube
250g rice noodles

For the kneidlach
2 eggs, lightly beaten
2 tablespoons oil or chicken fat
2 tablespoons soup stock or water
1 teaspoon salt
110g matzah meal or fine ground breadcrumbs

Place the chicken and the rest of the soup ingredients in a large pot, with enough water to cover. Bring it to the boil, then lower the heat and allow it to simmer for around 2 hours, topping up the water as necessary. Remove any fat that rises to the surface and keep to one side for the *kneidlach*.

Meanwhile, make the *kneidlach*. (Or you can buy them if you're super-busy!) In a bowl, stir together the eggs, oil or chicken fat, stock or water and salt, then add the matzah meal or breadcrumbs slowly until the mixture is thick. Cover and put it into the fridge for 30 minutes, then form into small balls.

Half an hour before serving, remove the chicken and set aside. Add the dumplings to the soup to cook for 30 minutes.

Meanwhile, shred the meat from the chicken and place into serving bowls – you can return the bones to the stock pot for extra flavour. Drop in the rice noodles, and let them cook for 2 minutes.

Gently place the noodles and the cooked *kneidlach* into the bowls with the chicken meat, cover with hot broth and serve piping hot to appreciative diners. Amazing!

Friday-night Dinner Roast Chicken and Yellow Rice

Pretty straightforward, though Nana always made it taste amazing. It was always the centrepiece of Friday-night dinner, and reminds me of home, family and comfort. I have so many happy memories of those dinners, memories I try to recreate today at my own table.

Serves 4
You'll need:

1 x 1.5kg whole chicken
2 tablespoons butter
1 lemon, halved
salt and pepper

For the rice
280g white long-grain rice
2 onions, peeled and chopped
2 tablespoons olive oil
2 teaspoons turmeric
A pinch of saffron
1/2 teaspoon salt
600ml water

Preheat the oven to 200°C/Gas 6. Place the chicken into a foiled roasting tin, rub the softened butter over the chicken and season generously. Put the cut lemon inside the chicken. Bung it into the oven and roast for 80–90 minutes. Stab it with a skewer: if the juices run clear, it's done. If not, put it back into the oven for another 10 minutes, then test again.

Half an hour before you want to serve, make the rice. Heat up the oil in a saucepan, add the chopped onion and cook for two minutes until starting to soften. Add the turmeric, saffron, salt and rice. Cover with the water and bring to a simmer for 8 minutes. Place a lid on top and turn the heat off. Leave the lid on until the rice is fully cooked and all the water is absorbed. Fluff with a fork and serve with the chicken. Enjoy!

Dad's Spicy Shepherd's Pie

I'll let Dad speak for himself here, as it's his recipe after all: 'I made this differently every time, but mostly it looks something like this. My spice mix varies according to how I feel on the day I'm making it, but I always have chilli, loads of chilli. My grandparents were Iraqi Jews who traded coffee in Burma. When the Japanese invaded they fled to Calcutta before moving to London in the 1950s. My heritage is where I get my love for spicy food, and I was always trying to share this with my children as they grew up.'

Serves at least 8, 'because that's how many I routinely had round my dining-table.'

You'll need:

2 tablespoons vegetable or coconut oil

500g lean lamb mince and Quorn

1–2 medium onions, peeled and finely chopped

1 stick celery, finely chopped

1 carrot, finely chopped

1 garlic clove, finely chopped

1 teaspoon chilli powder or 1 fresh chilli, deseeded and chopped

1 teaspoon ground cumin

200g frozen peas

1 tablespoon tomato purée

100ml vegetable or lamb stock

For the topping

500g sweet potatoes

600g potatoes

1 tablespoon milk

'I used half mince and half Quorn to make it healthier, and none of the kids ever noticed.' Heat half the oil. Fry the lamb mince and the Quorn together in the oil. Once the meat has browned, remove it from the pan and set it aside. Fry the onions in the remaining tablespoon of oil, until they are softening, about 5 minutes, then add the celery and carrot. Continue to fry for a couple of minutes, then add the garlic, chilli and cumin. Let them cook for a minute, then tip in the peas. Add the mince mixture with the tomato purée, and a little vegetable or lamb stock to moisten the mixture. Leave to cook for 5 minutes, then remove from the heat.

Preheat the oven to 200°C/Gas 6.

Meanwhile, peel and chop the sweet potatoes and the potatoes. Add them to a big pan of boiling salted water. When they are cooked, about 15 minutes, drain and mash them with the milk.

Tip the mince and vegetable mixture into a large greased baking dish, then smooth the potato mixture over the top. Put it into the oven for 35 minutes, until the top has browned.

'Hey presto – Spicy Shepherd's Pie!'

CHAPTER 6

Mum Guilt!

Zachary: 'Mummy …'

Me: 'Yes, Zach?'

Zachary: 'Can we please live in a tent?'

Me (spluttering on my bottle of water): 'Erm, why do you ask?'

Zachary: 'Because then you won't have to work and you can stay at home all day with us. We don't need new toys, we just need a tent so you can be with us.'

Bam! Mum Guilt, right there. It's inescapable and, it seems to me, inherent in any parent. Even if my rational mind knows we're better off with me working and building a future for them, I fold when one of my children says something like that. Within seconds I'm hastily reviewing all of my career choices and wondering if we *could* live in a tent – which, by the way, would be a disaster. Sorry, Zachary, but no. They'd soon regret it when it came to Christmas in the tent, and me having to say, 'Guys, no toys this year, but that's what you wanted.' Can you imagine their reaction?

I overthink everything when it comes to being a mummy. A prime example is at breakfast time. Most days the boys beg me to make dippy eggs. I have to leave for the *Loose Women* studio by 6.45 a.m. so I usually fob them off with a bowl of Weetabix before I run out of the door. Do I feel guilty? Hell, yeah. Do I also provide them with a strong female role model, a working mum supporting her family? Hell, yeah, to that too. But the doubts never go away.

Should I get up earlier to make dippy eggs each morning? No, I'd get tired, do my job badly, upset producers, shout at my kids, then not be able to pay the mortgage, but my head will still tell me I'm not a great mummy because I make the choices I make.

Some nights when the boys were younger, they'd both be asleep next to me in my bed, one on either side, while I worked on my laptop. Some people say that co-sleeping is bad as it makes children dependent, but others say it makes them feel loved and secure.

For us, it was a natural solution to make bedtimes easier when Zach and Leighton were younger. We all loved snuggling up together, and who's to say that was wrong? But I still doubted my decision: should I make them sleep in their own beds? I wondered. Have I messed them up mentally by letting them sleep with me? Loads of psychology books and the parenting advice you can read online strongly suggest that sleeping in the same bed with your children can be detrimental to their development. Well, not only do the boys and I thoroughly enjoy sleepovers in my bed, but at 3 a.m. when Leighton climbs out of his bunk bed to go for his early-morning pee, I'm not up for a debate as to where he then chooses to sleep. In with Mummy he comes. And my head still says: Should I force him to stay in his own bed?

The nagging goes on and on.

I don't do anything because a book or blog tells me to do it. I do it because it works for me. As long as I keep asking myself, Are they happy and healthy? I know, deep down, that things will be okay, that everything else is just fluff.

There is so much *opinion* out there. It's virtually impossible to escape other people's views, especially with so much online venting and so much advice readily available. It's becoming more and more difficult to decide how to parent as guilt is only a click away. I admit that when Zach asked me to give up work and live in a tent, I had a little sob. I explained to him that Mummy had to work to pay the bills and ensure we had a nice home. (Now we live with Joe, but I cover half of everything.) I made sure I let him know I love my work: I don't just do it for the money, it's also about my happiness as a mum. I want him to know he should never feel guilty for following his dreams and pursuing whichever career he will choose.

My children are at the heart of everything I do, and are better off with a happy, successful mummy as a role model. I get time off between jobs and throw myself into playing with my boys, but I also have days when I come home and I've got no energy left for them. That's okay too. Whether you're a stay-at-home or a working parent, what matters is that the situation is right for you and your family. No one else can make such an important decision for you.

Guilt isn't just a 'woman' thing. Fathers are faced with the same conflicts about work and quality time with their kids. My dad would have spent every second of every day playing with us if he could.

When I was asked if Zach would appear on *Big Stars, Little Stars* with me, I said, 'No.' I felt I was protecting him from an experience outside his comfort zone. However, Zach was adamant that he wanted to do it. I agonized over the decision. If I say no, will he think I'm ashamed of him? What if it's a huge amount of pressure on him? What if he doesn't like it? If he doesn't win, how will he react? Honestly, it was exhausting fielding my internal questions. That show is a competitive platform, which worried me. Would Zach feel 'less than' if he didn't win? I talked to him about it. I told him he could lose in front of a live audience, but he said he was fine about that. In the end I caved, and he had a great time. Zach didn't win but he loved it: he got to choose the charity we raised money for, and it taught him that we can help people through doing the silly stuff we do.

Another major source of Mum Guilt, for me, is Instagram or, more accurately, posting pictures of my boys on it. I love posting photos of us, but from time to time I'm accused of invading my boys' privacy. When this first happened, my reaction was 'Oh, gosh, I hadn't thought of it like that.' I decided to ask Zach and Leighton if they minded whenever I wanted to post up a picture: if they're not happy, I don't do it.

But why do I feel guilty about sharing gorgeous pictures of my boys? It wasn't so long ago that on a kid's twenty-first birthday all the embarrassing photos came out of photo albums for everyone to see. I guess we're always looking twenty years down the line to see if our kids will have any issues with love, affection, social skills as a result of the decisions we made as parents. I had the best parenting but I still went off the rails as a teenager.

Sometimes we forget that our children are their own individual selves. We feel we own them and that everything they do reflects on us, but everything I did in my crazy years reflected who *I* was, not my parents. They should bear no responsibility for my behaviour back then.

I know that I'm far from a perfect mum. For a start, I don't give the boys all-organic homemade food (I have a life). I didn't breastfeed them for years on end. (I hated breastfeeding but I gave it my best shot.) I breastfed Leighton for a few days but I knew I didn't want to carry on. I'd suffered post-natal depression after Zachary's birth and breastfeeding was partly to blame: I found it painful, exhausting and extremely demanding, so I stopped. Not breastfeeding made me better able to connect with my sons.

I don't have a routine that my children follow without a murmur. My working hours are sporadic so it would be difficult for us to keep to one. In any case, we like doing spontaneous things, which wouldn't happen if we stuck to a strict regime. I sleep with my boys, if they decide to crawl into bed with me. I get upset in front of them. (I'm human, not a robot.) And I'm okay with all of that. (Yay!) You're bound to do things differently from me, and that's okay too. We're happily imperfect, and we generally muddle through, like any other family, while I hope I'm making the right decisions. I'm so proud of my boys. When I look at them, I think I've done an amazing job without reading textbooks, each of which says something different. What is a perfect parent anyway? What does perfect parenting even look like?

As parents, we make decisions based on what we think is in everyone's best interest at the time. With hindsight we can often see what we might have done better, but what's done is done. Mistakes are inevitable.

We're human, yet we treat mums and dads like machines, giving them no room for error. For me, that started when I was pregnant with Zach. From the moment my bump showed there were pressures on me that I hadn't expected.

People always have an opinion on how you experience pregnancy, from whether you should go jogging or have an occasional glass of wine. People would come up to me and just rub my belly, like I was a metal Buddha! I felt my body had become public property with a child inside it, and that was where the Mum Guilt started.

Being a single mum made me grow up and become the person I am today. When Zachary was placed in my arms, I didn't feel anything, except hungry. I wanted to eat and sleep. I was overwhelmed by the task ahead of me, but I knew I wanted to be the best parent I could be. Having him, then Leighton, gave me the spur I needed to achieve the impossible.

So many people told me I wouldn't cope with a child when I was eighteen, but they failed to acknowledge that I was already making something of my life. I was the person I was, with or without my pregnancy. I was thrust into adulthood very quickly, and became a more multi-dimensional person, though any life experience can enhance who we are, not just having children. Undeniably, Zach and Leighton have made me much more than I was before they came into my life. Before they arrived, I didn't have a clue where my life was going. My dream was to become a singer, but without Zach, I don't know if I'd have kept trying.

Being a single mum can be difficult. Often we have no one else to lean on, no one to share the decision-making and responsibilities with. I cannot offer my children a conventional set-up, but who's to say that all of the love being thrown at them from every unconventional angle isn't exactly what they need?

Now that Joe and I have moved in together, we share the parenting. Joe is amazing with the boys, and an incredible father to his own son, but I'm fully aware that when it comes to mine the buck stops with me: Mum Guilt prevails.

I deal with it positively: I take my Mum Guilt and use it to question every decision I make that's related to my boys. I like weighing up all the arguments. Then I know my decisions are based on facts rather than gut feeling. Essentially, though, I still feel I'm stabbing in the dark when it comes to parenting. And I won't know for a long time, if ever, exactly what the results will be for my children of any decision I make, however well researched. I'm still learning to be okay with not knowing.

We are bombarded with 'experts' showing us how to be better parents. My advice is, unless you're looking for a specific answer to a dilemma, stay away. Put down the books, turn off your computer, and enjoy your children.

My style of 'mumdom' is pretty random, laid-back, and I'm just as likely to change my mind about the choices I make as go with them. I have to accept that I over-analyse everything I do for my kids. Then I look at the boys, and reflect: They're all right. They're good kids, happy, kind and healthy. I don't need them to be geniuses or top athletes, I'm happy the way they are: totally imperfect and totally amazing.

I've had some spectacular #parentingfails in my time. Not long after Zach was born, I was walking around a store, putting stuff in my basket. He was in his buggy and I'd placed the shop basket on top. At some point I'd lifted the basket to carry it on my arm and drifted off. About ten minutes later I was queuing at the till when I suddenly felt sure I'd had another basket or something. That 'something', of course, was Zach!

I don't think I've ever moved as fast as I did through that store. I ran up and down the aisles until I found him, parked by the mascara display, quite happy. It never happened again!

Another major #parentingfail: I had taken Zach to an amusement park and pre-warned him that he was going to be under five for payment purposes. At the kiosk, as soon as I told the lie, Zach insisted loudly, 'I'm not under five, I'm a big boy!' That'll teach me to try and save a fiver. The guy behind the till just looked at me, resigned, as if I was the fifth person he'd seen that day trying to pull off the same trick, and charged me the full whack.

Also, and this is a shameful reveal, I've been guilty of scaring my children to make them behave. That really is a major parenting fail, and something I swore to my parents as a child I would never do. It's amazing what you end up doing as a parent despite all your best intentions. When I was growing up, Mum and Dad would tell me stories of catastrophe and death relating to drug or alcohol use, or any kind of misbehaving. 'Did you hear what happened to Trevor? Well, he took one ecstasy tablet and died, just died.' No wonder I developed anxiety! I did the same to Leighton: 'Did you know what happened to the boy who lied to his mummy? Well, he had a terrible life and he had no friends.' Why did I say that? I was rumbled by Zach, who worked out that if the person in question had no friends, how would I know of their terrible fate? I couldn't answer that.

Because my boys had grown up mostly around me and my mum, there were certain things I hadn't taught them, such as standing up to wee. It was my sister's partner who showed them what to do at a fairly advanced age. It was a revelation for my sons, a terrible day for me. They felt like they'd grown a few inches, using the toilet like 'proper boys', but of course it meant more cleaning for me. I felt

I'd shirked my responsibilities as a mummy: I hadn't moved into the daddy zone of life skills. Of course, both boys would eventually have seen their peers doing it at school, but it was something I should have tackled earlier, with a packet of anti-bacterial wipes to make sure the toilet was pleasant for anyone (me) to use afterwards.

In everyday life, little parenting fails happen when I'm too tired to make the 'perfect' casserole, and instead throw a fish-finger sandwich at my children while insisting the ketchup is one of their 'five-a-day'. I could have made the fish fingers from scratch with fresh cod rolled in bread-crumbs but …

There's so much value to be had in believing in yourself as a parent. I find if I read too much about other parenting styles or trends, my confidence takes a knock. It's about trusting ourselves. Sometimes it's best just to keep plod-ding on, as long as everything is okay. I remind myself with each issue that comes up that I have the best interests of my child at heart, and that's what matters. It's impor-tant not to worry too much about what others are doing: there is no perfect way to bring up kids. If there was, we'd all be doing it!

Eventually, our children become adults, responsible for their own actions and decisions, and they will shape their own path in life, as I did. We don't have to do everything right all the time. Parenting isn't easy, whatever your set-up, so let's pat ourselves on the back. No, really, let's do it. We do an amazing job – and each of us does it in *our own way*. Each child is unique, with a unique set of circumstances, and we instinctively parent to the very best of our ability.

Try not to compare yourself to anybody out there. Let's be clear: no one is going to Instagram a picture of their freezer dinner, or their child having a meltdown in a supermarket because they weren't allowed one of those toys strategically placed at the front near the tills. Their photo from Disneyland isn't going to be one of them dragging the child out of a shop kicking and screaming because they weren't allowed any more candyfloss. They're not going to show you the pants they had to throw away because they'd forgotten to take their child to the toilet before a really long walk in the woods, and I've yet to see anybody post a video of themselves disowning their child by refusing to answer to 'Mum' after a particularly massive meltdown, all of which have happened in my parenting life.

I'm with Celeste Barber of #celestechallengeaccepted. I love her mockery of the perfection tsunami on Instagram, and the whole perfect-lives backlash online. People are questioning this stuff and wondering why real life isn't represented on social media. She makes me laugh. She's a legend, and others on the 'gram are challenging the #cleaneating phenomenon.

Rest assured that just because you don't see what other parents are going through, it doesn't mean they're not going through it!

Mum Guilt comes with the territory, except for those moments when we suddenly realize we've done something right. I had that with Zachary recently. I had a phone call from his teacher, and instantly said, 'Oh, no, what's he done?'

'Sorry to worry you but I had to ring you up and say Zach has been incredible today,' his teacher said. My jaw literally dropped. Not that I was shocked that Zach had done something amazing, just that it was recognized while he was at school. She told me they'd been to visit an old people's home: Zach had listened carefully, had had conversations with the residents and had even danced with one lady when they'd put on wartime music. It was one of my proudest moments as a mummy: my sons are kind, which means that everything I tell them is going in somewhere and working. Mum Guilt: bam! Gone.

STAY POSITIVE

Release Mum Guilt and get on with your life by recognizing that we only have to be good-enough, not perfect, parents. Decide if the guilt you're experiencing is warranted. Have you done something you feel isn't great in your parenting? If so, take steps to change the situation, if you can. Do some research, ask for help from trusted friends, and believe in your own innate ability to fix what's wrong.

Step away from people who make you feel guilty, and remember that we need to look after ourselves if we're going to parent our children effectively. Self-care is vital to an emotionally healthy home life. Trust in your choices: you decided to be a working mum or a stay-at-home parent for good reasons. Stand by those choices, and consider that any decision comes with negatives and positives. There's no such thing as perfect parenting.

CHAPTER 7

Recipes That Say Love (Version 2)

Leighton: 'Mummy ...'

Me: 'Yes, Leighton?'

Leighton: 'I don't want Weetabix, I want a dippy egg. *Pleeease*, Mummy! Please can you make me one?'

Me (knowing I won't have time to put my face on before my car collects me at 6.45 a.m. for *Loose Women* so I'll look like a sleep-deprived madwoman when I get there): 'Of course. Runny or squidgy?'

Food has so many good memories for me from my childhood that I want my sons to grow up with the same traditions. These recipes are super-easy, but they're all made with every bit of love I feel for my family.

Dippy Eggs

Allow one large egg each. Boil a saucepan of water, put in the eggs and set the timer for exactly 6 minutes for the right runny to squidgy yolk result.

Cut some slices of bread and butter them. We prefer wholemeal or granary. Don't toast it. Cut the slices in half, then into soldiers. Arrange on a plate.

Often I can't find the egg cups. They're like socks in our house. You know how socks go missing? They're not in the drawers or the washing-machine. It's the same with egg cups. They disappear from the cupboard and the dish-washer. So I just plonk the eggs on the plate, get a piece of kitchen roll to wrap round each one, because they're so hot, and, hey presto, dippy eggs! The delight on my sons' faces when they realize that's what they're having for breakfast is heart-warming.

Heart-shaped Birthday Eggs

Warning: these involve forcing down the heart-shaped egg rings in the pan as they don't frikkin' work very well! Everyone in my house gets a birthday breakfast with heart-shaped fried eggs. It's non-negotiable.

To recreate your own Solomon Birthday Treat, drizzle some oil into a frying pan. Grab your heart-shaped egg ring (available online), put it in the pan and crack an egg into it. Press it down while the egg is cooking or the white will leak out of the sides. I usually burn my fingers while I'm doing this, and often have to cook more eggs than we need to get it right!

All in all, it's quite hazardous, but my boys love it.

Wokcakes

These are really pancakes, but as I only ever use my wok to make them, I've christened them wokcakes. The bottom of the wok is smaller than a normal frying pan, so you can make tons of these beauties.

I always make them on special occasions and when the boys realize I'm making them, they run in and say, 'What's happened, Mummy?' because they know we're celebrating something.

You'll need:

2 large eggs
300ml milk
100g plain flour
oil, for frying

Mix together the eggs and milk in a bowl, then whisk in the flour until you achieve a smooth batter.

Heat the oil in the wok (if you don't have one, use a frying pan), then pour in a tablespoon of batter and swirl it around until it covers the base of the pan. Cook for about a minute on each side, then take the wokcake out of the pan and set it aside to keep warm. Repeat until you run out of batter!

Mine get eaten as I make them. We never have leftovers!

My kids always have a savoury wokcake first, with a ham and cheese filling, then the sweet ones. Zach's favourite filling is Nutella and banana, while Leighton likes lemon and sugar.

Mum's Yellow Fish Stew

I'm always worrying about getting enough fish into my boys' diets but this simple recipe my mum created does the trick. Zach and Leighton wolf it down!

Serves 4
You'll need:

1 side smoked haddock fillet, cut into chunks (roughly 400g)
2 potatoes, peeled and cut into small chunks
2 carrots, peeled and diced into small chunks
1 onion, peeled and diced into small chunks
3 sticks of celery, diced into small chunks
1 teaspoon fish seasoning herb mix
1 teaspoon turmeric
A pinch of salt
1 garlic clove, crushed (optional)

Fill a pan with 1 litre of water and bring to the boil. Add all of the ingredients together and simmer for around 30–35 minutes until the potatoes and fish start to soften and break down, giving a lovely intense flavour to the soup.

Serve piping hot with warm, crusty bread.

CHAPTER 8

Motherload

Motherload: *Come home. Prepare dinner. Shove the washing into the machine on the quickest setting. Iron and sort out the school uniform for the next day. Make sure homework's done, teeth are cleaned and bedtime happens at a not-too-outrageous hour, then flop onto the sofa, crack open the wine, and wonder if you can be bothered to go out on Friday night because it would mean the same again, but turbo-charged, and having to wash your hair ...*

Sounds familiar? If so, you're probably experiencing Motherload – a state of overload brought on by having expelled an infant or two from your private parts. At this point, you may want to grab a glass of wine and ignore the shouts of 'Mummy!' because you deserve some time out from the demands placed on us parents.

We love our children but, oh, trying to do everything 'right' can be tiring. Most evenings I wake up at 10 p.m.

on one son's bunk, having fallen asleep while I was putting them to bed. They don't seem to mind. They just think, Oh, she's gone again, settle down and go to sleep. I've usually got home late and shoved a lasagne into the oven while chatting with the boys. I've put the washing on, tidied up and set the table, so then we eat, watch a bit of telly and start the bedtime routine with a bath, story and bed. I'll make up the story, usually starring a six-year-old boy with fair hair who's really funny, bright, smart, lovely, and also, by some strange coincidence, has a name beginning with L. He will even have the same friends as Leighton. You can imagine how excited he gets when he realizes the boy might just be him!

As I'm talking I'll feel my eyelids getting heavy, though I sometimes think, This is comedy gold. I really should write children's stories. And suddenly it's ten o'clock and I've woken myself up with my snoring.

I don't know if that scenario rings a bell for you, but I'm guessing, whatever our careers or set-ups, it does. There's never quite enough time in the day to do everything on the to-do list. There's never quite enough time to do everything *properly*. In my heart of hearts, I want to cook homemade food for my children, and be there at bedtime every night, but the demands of my life mean that's just not possible.

When Leighton lost his first tooth he was staying with his dad. I was devastated not to be the Tooth Fairy. I felt I'd missed out on something really special.

When I lived in the *X Factor* house (because the filming schedule was so packed), I missed everything with Zach.

He took his first steps while I was away. He started saying proper words and stringing sentences together. I was heartbroken and I doubted that I was doing the right thing, yet staying with *The X Factor* was the best decision I've ever taken for me and Zach. It made me feel I could follow my ambitions as well as being a mummy. It was an important part of our development as mother and son – but it made me feel rubbish. I worried about whether he would run to me if he cut himself. Would he even know me? Would he still call me Mummy?

I was inside the *X Factor* house for twelve weeks. The producers took pity on me and allowed me to go home once a week because Zach was so little at just a year old. At that age so much changes so quickly. It was the little things that upset me, such as his laugh changing, and his choice of teddy bear being different from a week previously. I knew I had to grab the opportunities that lay in front of me, but it wasn't easy, and keeping positive about the experience became a real effort at times. I had to keep my eyes on the prize, and know that, whatever happened, I was doing it for my son. I had to focus on what I was trying to achieve, and remember how fortunate I was that I had a family who could help me get there by looking after my son – and doing the Motherload tasks in my absence.

The mental chatter, alongside all the physical and emotional tasks of Motherload, never stops but we can take steps to mitigate it. Most of us who have a career are continually worried about our work-life balance, yet working enriches my life, and gives me a sense of purpose that I'm happy to pass on to my sons. Choosing to go for it with *The X Factor* gave me a strong sense of the bond that existed between Zach and me. If it wasn't for him, I wouldn't have kept trying to succeed. I wanted to get somewhere in life, even at the cost of those precious months with my baby boy. In my eyes, what I achieved far outweighed the bits I missed, and I knew Zach was safe and happy with my mum and family.

Today, no one makes me feel I'm not a good-enough parent except myself. I spend a considerable amount of time away from my children so I make sure, these days, that when I come home the chores go out of the window. It's my backlash against Motherload, and the main way I offset the Mum Guilt. If I've been away all day the house-tidying can wait. I'd rather catch up with my boys and spend an hour building a den in the lounge than hoovering. I feel genuine joy if I build a good fort. Seriously.

I'll also shake it up a bit with some silly dancing. I'll put some music on and say, 'Look at me!' while I throw myself around. Best of all, though, is when Zach and Leighton say they're going to do a show. They hide in the corridor, whispering about what each will do, and Zach is always the compère, introducing the production. I love it when I have time to ignore my list and play with them. Sometimes we stand round the piano, me playing and the boys singing. They love Justin Bieber songs, and the chatter in my brain about chores and work fades away as they belt out their favourites. Zach does an amazing rendition of Bruno Mars's 'Just the Way You Are'. Major proud-mummy moment. When I see them smile, the whole world stops, for a moment, and I know that whatever I'm doing, it's right.

Perhaps you kick a ball round the garden with your child or children, do some crafts or watch their favourite telly show with them. Whatever it is, it shows them they are way more important than the to-do list!

Because of the career I'm in, I never know when I'm going to work. There is no guarantee I'll be asked to do telly work for ever so I do pretty much everything I'm asked to do, which, of course, leads to massive Mother-load. I need to save enough money to support my family whatever happens in the future. It's my choice not to have a stable job, but now and then I realize I need to spend more time with my boys so I make sure I don't over-commit.

I have a problem with saying no. I love making people happy, which generally involves saying yes. Saying no is a powerful way of dealing with Motherload. 'No, I can't iron your shirt while making a lasagne'; 'No, I can't help you with your homework because (a) it's yours, and (b) I need to make a call for work.' I learnt how to deal with my urge to agree to everything by giving myself permission to refuse. Really, it was so hard at first! It's my people-pleasing side: I have to recognize that, then take action. Now if someone asks me to do something, instead of blurting out, 'Yes,' straight away, I ask for time to consider it – a bit of breathing space: 'Can I do this?'; 'Do I want to do this?'; 'What is the cost of saying yes?'

When it comes to family, I've never had a problem with tuning in to what's really important. When my sister got married, I turned down every bit of work so I could get to her wedding. My family is the most important part of my life, full stop. I'm working for them but I mustn't neglect them. That would be totally counterproductive.

I worry about technology. It may be a relief when the boys are zoning out on computer games while I get the ironing done, but gaming comes with its own issues. Most parents I know are anxious about the impact of games like Fortnite on their kids, because violence is inherent in them. We worry that it might adversely affect our children, and about how insular they are when they're absorbed in a video game. I wouldn't let Zach play Fortnite, until I realized his mates had this new dimension to their friendship. It was a sociable way of connecting and I wanted to acknowledge that rather than condemning it outright. I tried it myself so I'd I know what I was letting us both in for, and this was what happened.

My eldest: 'Can I download Fortnite?'

Me: 'No.'

My eldest: 'All my friends have it and play and I'm the only one who can't play.'

Me: 'Let me play it and see.'

Zach goes to bed

I'm now two hours in, dressed as some kind of raven, on my way to Tilted Towers with three people I don't know.

#mummyfail.

I discovered that Fortnite is near-addictive but all of the games are built that way. And children need a tech-based education because the jobs of the future will be available to them only if they're tech-literate. They need to consume technology to learn about it. I want my boys to be tech-savvy, but I also want to protect them, which makes for an interesting tension.

Most important to me was that Zach, and now Leighton, wouldn't be isolated from the friends they had made who were playing Fortnite. Most of Zach's friends communicate via gaming, and who's to say that's wrong? When he left school, about which more later, I decided to let him play so that he could connect with his mates. Motherload is about choices: I can choose to take on too much and be overwhelmed, or I can be pragmatic about something like Fortnite. At the end of the day, I combat overwhelm by asking: Is it right for us as a family? That takes the heat out of the situation. I look at each issue objectively, and then I can make a clear choice.

I imagine you have your own feelings about that game. Perhaps you've decided not to let your child play it. And that's fine. We all exercise control, which isn't always easy.

Gaming isn't a clear-cut issue, but I stand by my choice. It takes me out of Motherload and leaves me feeling I have the freedom to act in a way that's best for us as a family right now.

I keep talking to Zach and Leighton about gaming and its effects on their brains. I communicate with them openly about the issues that worry me. I experience Mum Guilt over allowing them to play computer games, yet while they're playing I have time to get stuff done.

I worry, too, about whether I'm overprotective of my boys. My parents let me walk to and from primary school on my own. I wouldn't dream of letting Zach and Leighton do that, even though child abductions are no more prevalent now than they were when I was at school.

What's that about? Are we really less safe now? I don't know the answer to that. I want my children to be safe, but I also want them to be streetwise and independent. I wonder if being overprotective of our children does them a disservice?

There is so much to cause overload, these days, from worries about children's freedom to the practical tasks we perform each day to keep our families thriving. I combat it by ditching the least essential tasks, like hoovering or dusting, and focus on creating brilliant memories.

Every day is a gift. I don't know what's going to happen, ever, so I try to enjoy every second. I'm clear that I want to be an old woman, surrounded by my sons and their children, reminiscing about the fun we had. In fact, we do it now. When I get round the table with my family, we relive all our best memories.

Memory-making can be a conscious thing: some mornings if I'm awake before the boys I'll jump on their beds and tickle them to wake them up. I can be sitting chatting when suddenly I'll do something crazy to make them laugh. If they're in the shower I'll turn the hot tap off so that the water runs cold. If they're in the bathroom I'll sneak up and turn the light off. It's silly stuff, but it helps me forget the overload and brings me back into the present moment. I don't schedule quality time because that would simply add to my Motherload.

Our evenings currently look something like this: I get home, clear up the cat sick on the floor, empty the litter trays, bleach everywhere, realize I forgot to buy mince on the way home, rummage through the freezer for something for dinner, cajole the boys into eating their veg, squabble over the TV control, shove all three of us into the shower, tell them to clean their teeth and get their PJs on, read that night's story, wake up at 10 p.m., and crawl into bed without removing make-up or false eyelashes. Wake up to the sound of my alarm. Start again.

Overload is a challenge: we can cave in under the weight of everything we haven't done, or we can offload some of it by choosing what to prioritize. Let's be honest about the things that are important to us. It's important to me to create a happy, playful vibe at home. It's wildly imperfect, but it makes us wildly happy, and knocks Motherload out of the box.

And who's to say we're not already perfect as parents? Are we so fixated on one version of perfect that we fail to see the positive in our way of doing things? Aren't there millions of examples of perfect parenting in millions of different circumstances? Isn't the perfect parent one who unconditionally loves their children, in whatever form that love presents itself?

Motherload – or Parentload, as I should probably call it – affects all of us, but it doesn't have to rule our lives. We get to decide what we want to worry about, and what we have to let go to have a career and home life that works for us.

STAY POSITIVE

When Motherload threatens to overwhelm you, remember this: when you're on your death bed (hopefully, a long time from now), surrounded by family and friends, the stuff you'll remember won't be the completed to-do list, it'll be the fun and laughter. Changing the state of mind that comes with Motherload – stressed, overwhelmed, overworked – isn't easy but giving up trying to be perfect is rewarding.

Start to create those memories, and change that mindset. Book a trip. Fly a kite. Take some time in nature together. Kick a few autumn leaves, throw snowballs, dig sandcastles together. Ask yourself, how much will I gain by sticking to my to-do list? Let yourself forget about the housework, the washing, the home-prepared food, and instead spend time together, just enjoying each other's company.

CHAPTER 9

Creating a Happy Family Vibe

Let's get something straight. I haven't always had a happy, fun-filled family life. There have been times in the past when I've been in a relationship where someone has projected their insecurities onto me. I could have taken a negative standpoint about it, but chose to make it into a positive. I did this by becoming really aware of what I wanted in my close family environment. I thought, I need to work out how to create something that's the exact opposite of what I've got. I had my experience of growing up in a loving family to contrast with what I was going through. It helped me to regain my sense of self, and make decisions about how I wanted to live. It wasn't easy.

To give my sons the happiness they deserved, I had to grow up and take responsibility for the environment I'd created for them, which meant I had to make difficult choices about who I was with. When I discovered I could create my own family environment, I felt a sense of freedom and lightness. Hooray for me! I could enjoy my family life by doing it *my* way. Now I have a settled home life and my boys are happy and healthy, though they have their moments, like all children!

Having siblings helped. As children, we made fun out of the silliest things, and I loved that. Most days we engineered big belly-laughs, which became my absolute favourite thing. Being able to mess about and see the funny side of normal stuff has carried me through my hard times. In fact, a good belly-laugh is the ultimate secret to our happy family vibes. We're all idiots, and I include my boyfriend Joe in that, of course. It's why we love hanging out together. It really works. What could be simpler than laughing as a way to de-stress from Motherload, Perfect Parenting and Mum Guilt? It's a no-brainer.

Let's not forget that stress is a normal response to life's challenges. We can't get rid of it, but we can identify the things that cause us worry and, in recognizing them, work on changing them. It's not always possible. For example, I'm always late. Always. I never seem able to arrive anywhere on time because I take on too much. I can choose to do something about that. I can cancel unnecessary jobs or commitments. I could also get up earlier and go to bed later but I'm not sure what effect that would have on my ability to contribute to the show I'm doing, so perhaps not!

I'm learning to delegate. My mum now helps with some of my PR stuff, and often with childcare or shopping, which helps me to relax and choose to have fun. When I see my sons laughing, holding their stomachs, I instantly focus on what's important: their happiness. Nothing is permanent, except the love we have for each other, and life is short. That knowledge reminds me not to take my sons for granted: every day they get a little older while our family changes and grows. Nothing stays the same, except our ridiculous sense of humour, of course.

To give you an example of our totally hilarious (to us) in-family jokes, Joe does this gross thing with the boys. He tells the boys to pull his finger, and when they do, he farts. Childish, and wildly funny (to the boys – and probably me too, if I'm honest!).

Seconds earlier, the boys might have been ripping each other's hair out (they're brothers, after all), yet something as simple as Joe's gag makes them stop and laugh together. When I look at them laughing and clutching their tummies, I know they'd do anything for each other. Moments of light relief really help me remember our family's love. Perhaps you don't have our sense of humour (I wouldn't blame you!), so create that can't-breathe laughter in some other way, whether it's watching a comedy or finding funny YouTube posts.

The boys aren't saints. They fight, or they're grumpy. When that happens, I look at whether they're hungry, tired or bored. If it's any of those three things, it can be easy to fix. If it's something more nebulous, I take time out and focus on them to discover what's rattled them.

It's important to have solid boundaries in place and that's been a struggle for me at times. My boys test the limits all the time. It's part of growing up, and I respect that, but I draw the line between what's acceptable and what's not. I look at where I may have let the boundaries slip, perhaps in allowing later bedtimes so they're tired, or if I've been working too hard so they're missing my attention.

Whatever it is, I try hard to recognize my part in the situation. That isn't always possible. Zach and Leighton have their own personalities and moods that are affected by different things, so there's a limit to what I can achieve if one or other of them is grumpy. Sometimes it's about giving extra cuddles or spending special time together away from my work pressures. Often, that's the key to reconnecting and getting our day back on track.

Letting the kids run naked now and again works wonders in upping the happiness quota. Zach and Leighton love flinging off their clothes as soon as the weather gets warm, but they do it in winter too. I bought them both cute lumberjack pyjamas, but five minutes after I'd forced them to wear them, they were wrestling in their pants on the bedroom floor, like two Mowglis from *The Jungle Book*, which made me laugh, and definitely relaxed them.

I love a practical joke as much as they do, especially when I'm not the one on the receiving end. In our new house, we love a good game of hide and seek – there are so many nooks and crannies which make great hiding places and the boys love it when I jump out and frighten them half to death. We all end up in a heap on the floor, laughing.

I'm proud of how hard I work to create a laughter-filled, loving home for my boys. They come first in my life. (Joe comes last, but he knows it!) I love hanging out with them and often have the most fun when we rock up at a toy shop. I can play cowboys or pirates in the aisles for hours.

Finding time to unwind is good for family vibes. Leighton and I like doing a bit of yoga or Pilates together on the lounge floor. We do a fifteen-minute session in the morning by choosing a class online. Leighton gets really excited when he can do a posture properly. I like getting out to do a class, too – I'm glad when I've done one. It refocuses my mind and helps me to find perspective, especially if there's any dissent at home.

One thing I don't do is I don't schedule in quality time because that would make it yet another thing to have to do. I don't want to create stress over how much fun we're having together, because that would be totally counter-productive. You can't plan for fun. You can't schedule happiness, but you can choose to create it. Not arguing with your partner is always a good start. Not forcing the children to do something they don't want to do when they're tired is another good way to create a happy home vibe. There are so many ways in which we can take our foot off the accelerator at home, and build in little bits of relaxation.

Every family is different. There are different dynamics, different tensions, perhaps even relatives who don't speak to each other, or issues from childhood that are yet to be resolved. Each family usually has some kind of tension rumbling along inside it so a happy vibe all the time isn't possible. Regardless of how positive my family life is, there are unresolved extended-family issues. That's normal, and most of us experience it at some point, especially when you're a single parent.

My main way to combat stress and enjoy my life is simply to appreciate it, even if the day hasn't gone the way I planned it. When we're eating dinner together, I ask the boys about the best bits of their day, and I tell them mine. It's a small way of finding the nugget of gold that might be buried in stress and worry. I'm touched by the small stuff, like when Joe pours me a glass of water without me asking, or Leighton goes downstairs and turns the lights off at bedtime so I don't have to do it.

That's the stuff that makes me feel warm and fuzzy. The good bits are often little things, a smile from a neighbour or colleague, a funny text from a friend, the smell of rain, or sunshine on my face. Noticing such things can change how I feel, and help me get back to my happy state: so many good things happen every day, so many chances to appreciate beauty or nature, but they are often pushed out by stress. It sounds obvious, but noticing them helps me to keep a sense of perspective. When the children are playing up, or I can't get home in time to make dinner, or I've heard some bad news, I try to focus on what I'm grateful for, and it always comes back to my imperfect family, my tribe. Being a parent is the best thing in my world, and I'm so thankful to be a daughter, sister, aunty and friend as well.

No matter how many wet towels are draped on the floor, how much peanut butter is smeared on the table or how many wet swimming trunks left on their beds, I know I'll love my boys whatever happens. I know that every day is a gift. Appreciating every moment is so important. Even when the boys are replaying the Second World War and the rice boils over, I remember that this day will never be repeated. Breathing and counting to ten help me rebalance if I feel things are running away from me. Counting my blessings helps when things feel out of control, or I've been snappy.

I'm still working out my parenting dos and don'ts. It takes time, practice and a few mistakes to find out what suits us, and that's fine. Life is messy, and parenting is part guesswork, part logical thinking, part emotional roller-coaster, and that's okay too. These days, I do what feels right with my kids, even though someone looking into our house would probably think I'm a total loony.

Creating your own vibe is an adventure, an exploration of what fits and what tickles you and your brood. Risk looking silly. Enjoy every second of having fun with your people, and understand that we don't have to have a perfect home life. There are always stresses and strains: money might be tight or time an issue.

Most parents I know are racing from work to the school run, to homework and arranging social lives, interests and dealing with all their domestic tasks.

Perhaps take time to stop, breathe, watch a funny DVD together, tell a few jokes and make an effort to reconnect with the people who you love the most, and who love you too.

STAY POSITIVE

Create memories. Let's all make having fun together at home the top priority (after food, sleep and clothing needs are catered for!). Let's enjoy our children, our relatives and friends by remembering that the time to create happy memories together is *now*.

Practise filling your home with love: make a conscious effort to show your family – biological or otherwise – how much you love them every day.

There are laughter clubs and laughter yoga classes. Do whatever it takes to enjoy the benefits of a good giggle, boosting mood and health.

Showing affection isn't always easy, especially after a hard day at work, but it's worth it. Not only does it foster greater intimacy with your partner or spouse, but it strengthens the happy vibe in the home. Keep it as part of your everyday routine, making every day a new opportunity to show your love.

CHAPTER 10

Perfectly Imperfect

Self-esteem. It's a biggie, isn't it? It lies under everything we are as a person. It's the word that sums up our sense of ourselves, whether we genuinely like or love ourselves, and who we are. It takes in our looks, our attitudes, our behaviours and personality. And without it, we suffer. We can fall short of our potential. We can be unkind to ourselves. We can judge ourselves on what others are saying or thinking of us. We can believe it's only our looks that make us lovable. Everything we can achieve in life comes down to self-esteem.

So, do we have enough, and if not, how do we get some more?

It's a question I'm not sure I can answer. It's something we develop as a child, in our family environment, with the people who keep us safe. For some of us, self-esteem comes naturally, but for many others, it can be elusive, something we have to nurture in ourselves as adults, forgiving ourselves for being the way we are, and learning self-care as a way of being.

What I know for sure is this: self-esteem does not come with our appearance. It is not dictated by others who judge our bodies, telling us if we're pretty, ugly, fat, thin, wobbly, saggy or perky.

I have a flawed and unique body. It's far from perfect, and I love it because it's mine. I have never hated my body. I spent the majority of my youth feeling pretty confident and good enough. School had been difficult when it came to fitting in with my appearance, but my personality won out and in the end I had a blast. It is only when somebody says something isn't right, that 'good enough' becomes 'good enough?' It happened to me when I was on holiday with my elder son a couple of years ago. I've never been one to call the paps because, quite frankly, I can't think of anything worse than my private holiday being taken up with a photo shoot. Holidays with my family are sacrosanct. However, somebody managed to find us and secretly take pictures of us on the beach. I was wearing a mismatched strapless bikini with my hair screwed up on top of my head. I had hairy legs and wasn't wearing make-up, which, let's be absolutely clear, didn't bother me in the slightest because I'm happy with the way I look. While playing bat and ball in the sea with my son, I was papped. I still have no idea where the photographer was hiding.

Much to my surprise, this became national news. It must have been a really slow summer for the tabloids! Seeing myself in a newspaper article surprised me because I was under the impression that no one knew where I was. I wasn't shocked or horrified by what I looked like. It was only when I read the headline and the picture captions that I started to question my appearance, purely in response to what was being said about me. I was being body-shamed.

Before I read that article, I was blissfully unaware of what anyone might think about my image. Honestly, I just didn't think about it, so I assumed no one else would. Naïve? Possibly.

It became apparent that whoever had written that article thought I'd got the holiday look completely wrong. The saddest part of the piece was they could have told me I'd got it wrong with my bikini but, no, it was because of my body.

You can change a bikini if you want to. Bikinis don't have feelings! But it wasn't my bikini that was 'at fault': it was how saggy my boobs looked in it. I can't change them – and I don't want to – so why was someone telling me they are a #fail? How can something that's a part of me, that makes me *me*, be wrong? The part of my body that breastfed my children is attached to me, has never upset me, so why did it upset them? For the first time, I questioned the power the media has over us in telling us how we 'should' look.

It was all so ridiculous. I found it funny, but the article's message was disturbing. It was absolutely clear: if you don't look a certain way, you're failing at life. If your body doesn't resemble a certain narrowly defined type, you're not good enough. I was being compared to somebody else.

Somehow the newspaper felt it was okay to pit two very different women against each other, saying that if you look like her it's okay, but if you look me, it's not. I wouldn't normally care that much about someone else's opinion, but the article wasn't just about me: it could have had an effect on women everywhere. For anyone to be body-shamed affects us all because it tells us, not so subtly, how we *should* look and how we *shouldn't*.

Since when was it wrong to be imperfect? We're all imperfect. I'm guessing the journalist who wrote that story has their own imperfections.

That was when I started questioning the media's impact on women's self-esteem and our perceptions of our bodies. It really hit home. The constant subliminal messages we receive are telling us we aren't good enough, and that's not okay. I decided to let that particular paper know that I'm happy in my body, and I refuse to be part of that narrative.

I wanted to turn what might have been a major negative into a massive positive (yay!). I know it shouldn't take a personal attack to make me think about the bigger picture, but it opened my eyes to the scrutiny women endure.

It really upset me that other women like me are being made to feel ashamed of their bodies. I called out the paper on social media, tweeting: 'I LOVE MY BODY. My boobs are a result of being pregnant & breastfeeding & I love them. I'm just as sexy as [the woman I was pitted against].' Later, I posted a picture of me and my boys, with the caption: 'Currently swinging my saggy maggies around the pool on holiday with these two'.

Making fun of it was my way of taking away its power.

Don't get me wrong, bits of my body are a bizarre mystery to me. For example, why are my toe hairs longer than my eyelashes? How could Nature have imagined that would benefit me? Yet I refuse to hate myself. In fact, I love my body's quirky bits – and there are plenty of them, I can tell you. I've got saggy boobs, hairy legs (most of the time) and a pair of delightful muffin tops over my knickers that mean I can lie on any surface and be perfectly comfortable and insulated.

Totally imperfect.

Seeing myself being compared so blatantly made me want to speak out. I'm in a privileged position. I have a platform on social media that allows me to reach lots of women (and men) to spread the message that, actually, we're all pretty much okay as we are. I'm also now a *Fabulous* magazine columnist, which is a major turn-around – and I've written about skinny-shaming, when people who are very slim, like my sister Jemma, get told they need to eat more.

In our society, we're conditioned to believe that one body type equals pretty, and the rest therefore needs fixing. We idolize size zero, which allows corporations to try to sell us things we think we need to get that bit nearer to perfection.

We know that buying a particular shampoo won't give us the same hair as the model in the advert and that a certain razor won't give us the legs we see in the picture.

I'll do everything I can to remind people that it's all just marketing. We can choose to have fun with our appearance and change it, but there's no such thing as perfection. We're all perfectly imperfect, so forget the so-called 'flaws': let's focus on the amazing bodies, faces, brains and personalities we *do* have. Don't you think that seeing models of all different shapes, colours, sizes and genders on the catwalk would be an amazing way to celebrate our individuality and diversity? I like who I am, so the idea of making someone uncomfortable in their own skin doesn't feel right. Don't tell me that only a tiny percentage of the population has any hope of looking good.

I see beauty as a state of mind. We're all beautiful and we're all imperfect, and it's because of those imperfections that we're interesting, varied and attractive. Like most young people, I grew up exposed to society's ideals of what is pretty, cool or acceptable. I read *Smash Hits* and saw all the skinny, beautiful girls in there. I watched TV and consumed other magazines. The subliminal message was always 'You have to look like this, do this, be this, in order to be good enough'.

Thank God I didn't grow up in the age of social media. Nowadays, young people are bombarded by a slew of 'perfection', whether it be looking amazing, wearing the right clothes, having the coolest friends or the ideal family. With more access to the media, young people have an uphill battle to gain self-confidence.

That's why I want to celebrate, loudly, my imperfections in the hope I can counteract those messages. I've given birth twice, and have the scars to prove it. I wouldn't get rid of my stretchmarks even if I could. Seriously. They chart where I've stretched and shrunk through and after my pregnancies. My favourite is the smiley-face stretch-mark – it's like an upturned smile running from under my tummy, along my bikini line and back up again. I'm a human emoji!

My muffin tops are perfectly natural. We women get them because of our oestrogen levels. Oestrogen makes us store fat in the tummy, thigh and bum areas. It's a medical fact, so why should we feel ashamed? Where is it written that women should feel disgust at this?

No one should make any of us, women or men, feel ashamed of our bodies. I feel just as sexy as an eighteen-year-old in a bikini – and I want everyone out there to feel the same. I laughed when I saw that article because I'm happy enough in my own skin not to take it too seriously. I didn't need a national newspaper to approve of my body but I couldn't help asking myself, Should I care what they think?

The answer was a resounding '*No!*' I absolutely don't. My family did care, though. My dad took it to heart, and I realized it isn't just us who are affected by that kind of public comment: it's all of us. I care deeply that we women are being told we're not good enough, not 'perfect' enough, if we have the audacity to wear a bikini after the age of eighteen! This is what a normal woman's body looks like. Get used to it! We have saggy boobs, marks left by our pregnancies, lines on our faces as we get older and wiser – and none of these things is shameful. I don't really exercise, apart from manically hoovering the house now and then, and carrying my children over the years, but, yes, I put in hair extensions. Yes, I wear make-up. Yes, I wear push-up bras. But I genuinely love myself without that stuff, and I really want to encourage you to love yourself as you are, regardless of your beauty or fitness regime.

I walked into a salon once and was told by the beautician that I should try Botox, at the age of twenty-eight, 'before it's too late'. I was so shocked I walked straight out. There are so many opportunities for us to feel bad about ourselves. We have to reject that pressure, and tell ourselves we're fine as we are in all our imperfect glory. Then body image becomes more about developing your self-esteem, by telling yourself, 'Hold on, you're pretty frickin' amazing!' I've shared 'before' and 'after' photos of myself, photographed as I am in a bikini, then Photo-shopped into the finished image for a magazine. The edited photo was thinner *and* curvier than the real me, and my skin looked polished and smooth. Cut to real life, and my wobbles were back, my skin looked so-so – but my smile was just as wide.

I love exposing that stuff. Images manipulated with airbrushing or filters should be labelled as such, so we all know that the look is unachievable, a work of art or fantasy. Then there's nothing wrong with it: it becomes something we like to look at, rather than an impossible ideal to try to achieve.

I don't accept that everybody on *Love Island* is the epitome of beauty. I can find someone attractive without knowing what they look like. If I'm attracted to someone, I'm engaged in communicating with them. I don't take in superficial things, like what they're wearing. In some parts of Africa, the woman who can hold the biggest basket on her head is deemed the most beautiful. In Tudor times, the fashion was for white skin and a tiny waist. It's all just flippin' fashion! It has no relation to real people living interesting, happy, meaningful lives. It's who you *are*, not what you look like that's important. Every element of your being constitutes your beauty, not what's on the surface.

We've all known people who are unattractive because of who they are. Doesn't matter if they're stunningly beautiful, if they're selfish or mean. So, let's rip up the rule book that says big boobs, big bums and flat tummies are the only definition of beauty. I don't accept it – and neither should you. Trust me, every element of your being is beautiful. You were created from stardust. Every atom in this universe is stardust, and you can't get more beautiful than that.

Start to hold people accountable for the things they say to you and about you. If somebody says something mean or negative about you, your body or your appearance, question it. Don't be afraid to challenge social norms and ideals. No one has the right to tell you how to feel about your body, so when they try to, don't let it go lightly.

Find a way to feel good about your body. For me, it's realizing that my body serves a purpose and I have the utmost love and respect for it. When I look in the mirror, I see me. I don't see stretchmarks, saggy boobs, muffin tops, a wonky nose and spots – I just see me. Even if my body changes, whatever I see before me is still me. It's always going to be me.

And if all of the above fails, just believe that you're beautiful and you won't even notice what other people think. Believe that you're enough, that you're beautiful and everything you always wanted to be, and everyone who questions it will be deflected by the forcefield of your conviction. I bet most people will go along with it anyway – and so they should!

If you feel beautiful inside, it radiates on the outside. Do whatever you have to do to like yourself, and the rest will follow.

STAY POSITIVE

I'm incredibly privileged to be able to help a charity called ChildLine. It offers counselling to children and young people via a helpline. I talk to youngsters struggling with self-confidence, and they often worry about their looks, but it soon becomes obvious that there's so much more to their low self-esteem: it's deep-rooted.

Similarly, if you aren't happy about your looks, it's worth delving a bit deeper to find out why you feel that way or who might be making you feel 'less-than'.

Get help from a professional if you need it. Ask your friends to give you personalized pep talks. Try talking yourself up, saying really nice things to yourself, commenting on how amazing you look today, even if you don't yet believe it.

Write a list of everything you like about yourself. It might be something like 'I love my third eyelash from the right', but do it. Seeing all the brilliant things about our bodies and minds written out can start the rebuilding process. Self-esteem is fragile, but we can all work at it. Remember that most people are not judging us: they're too busy judging themselves to worry about anyone else.

CHAPTER 11

Hairy McLary

J oe: 'What are you doing, Stace?' He is visibly shocked.
   Me: 'I'm putting glitter on my leg hairs. What does it look like?'

Joe (blank horror on his face): 'Course you are, Stace. Let me know when the bathroom's free.'

Me: 'I might be a while. I still have to colour them in with special mascara for *Loose Women*.' I can hear the excitement in my voice at my brilliant plan to vajazzle my luscious long leg hair.

Joe walks away silently, shaking his head.

As you've probably gathered by now, I'm not fussed about hair removal. You'd think that what I just said was a revelation of earth-shattering proportions, judging by the backlash – and support – I get on social media when I show off pictures of my hairy legs.

I'll go even further: I haven't shaved my bush in ten years, and I rarely bother shaving my legs, even when I'm on holiday. Now, as you know, I'm part-Yeti. I don't have fair hairs that are barely there. I have proper dark thick glorious hair on my legs, in my pits and on my womanly bits. Yes, I'm hairy. (EXTREME SHOCK! HORROR!) At school, I was called 'Hairy McLary from Donaldson's Dairy'. At the age of ten! It's amazing how a bit of body hair can be so controversial.

What exactly is the problem?

People are deeply offended by female hair in general (except the hair on our heads. We're allowed that, apparently). In adverts for razors, women pretend to shave already-shaved legs! What's that about? Is the alternative – a hairy female leg – just too offensive to show?

I'm so hairy that if I want smooth legs I have to shave them every day. How boring would that be? I have a five o'clock shadow ten minutes after whipping the razor out. Do you remember those Play-Doh toys we had as children, the ones where the Play-Doh squeezed out to make pretend hair? Well, that's me. As soon as I've shaved, the hairs are squeezing back out.

When I turn up at the *Loose Women* set, I'm surrounded by quite a few post-menopausal women. Their hair doesn't grow as much so they're pretty smooth. When they see me, their reaction is generally: 'Oh, my God, your leg hairs are insane!' And they are. Because I sit at the desk on *Loose Women* I can be like the Abominable Snowman underneath it because no one watching TV can see my legs.

One day my producer said to me: 'Stace, why don't we do a topic on shaving, or not shaving to be exact? Can you bear not to shave for a whole month?'

I replied: 'You don't even have to ask me. I probably wouldn't have shaved anyway!'

So, I left my leg hair to grow in abundance and by the end of the month it was really long, much longer than Joe's. That was when I thought the best way to show it off would be with some glitter and coloured mascara. *Let's vajazzle them!*

People were disgusted.

'Ugh, you're so dirty!' was one comment.

'My God, woman, shave your legs!' was another.

Nobody says Joe, or any other man, is disgusting for having hairy legs, so why women? Hair is as natural to us as it is to men. Seriously, I just don't get why it's such a problem for people: it's obvious the hair is meant to be there. My reaction was, 'The joke's on you [the haters] because it's winter and I'm warm. I'm insulated by body hair.'

Shaving every day really is such an effort. My legs are so long that I'd have to do yoga poses to reach my ankles – the tricky bits – in the shower. I generally miss them, leaving a fuzzy cuff on my ankles and knees. I have so much hair – one long string running from my pubes to my legs, which means it'd be a full-time job to depilate.

On holiday, I'm generally with my family, who couldn't care less if I'm hairy or not. I guess people might be thinking, Ugh, put your pubes away, but I really don't care if my lady garden is hanging out. When I visited Australia to surprise Joe in 2017, I did everything, my hair, nails, fake tan, but totally forgot to shave. It was so funny being on the beach in Oz with all the young people and teenagers: I was the only one with body hair. Honestly, the looks I got!

It's all about conditioning. As women, we're conditioned to shave. We grow up believing that we're not attractive unless we remove our body hair. We grow up thinking hair is just a man thing, yet it happens to every single woman in the world. How can this be offensive?

At school during a particularly cringy sex-education lesson, we learnt about the birds and the bees. The teacher put on a video, which showed a full-frontal man with pubic hair. Silence. No reaction. A woman appeared with a full bush and kids were saying, 'Yuck' or 'Disgusting' and 'Shave ya bush'. We wouldn't react like that to any other part of our bodies! Can you imagine people saying, 'Ugh, breasts! Put 'em away'?

Pubic hair is a funny one. I felt embarrassed in that lesson because I had pubes and was wondering if I was dirty. Was I gross? I was ten, for Heaven's sake!

I'm not trying to take a stand for feminism by avoiding the razor. You can be a feminist whether you shave or not. The concept is about equal rights for women and men. I feel that it's about *you* deciding for *yourself* if you want to be smooth, without being *pressured*. That's what needs to change.

Ruth from *Loose Women* loves her fuzz-free legs, and there's nothing wrong with that. I just think that no one has the right to tell us what to do – whether it's advertisers or feminists.

Again, it's about making choices. I could get up ten minutes earlier each day to do my pins, but do I want to eat breakfast or shave? For me, there's no contest: breakfast wins every time.

So much of the shaving debate chimes with body-shaming and body-positivity trends. I would like to see a world in which women aren't shamed into shaving, and instead can step back, look at the process objectively and decide, without pressure, whether they want to shave or not. As we grow more confident in ourselves, whatever our shapes, sizes and hair situations, I hope we can bring body positivity to hair removal.

Overcoming the pressure to shave comes with realizing whose opinions you really care about. When I first met Joe, I shaved a bit because I thought it was expected of me. How could he possibly find me attractive if I was hairy? When I realized he finds me attractive with or without hair, I questioned who I was shaving for.

I'm lucky that Joe grew up with three women. There were no men in his life past the age of eleven. He has a lot of respect for and empathy with women. His incredible mum raised him and his two sisters on her own, so he doesn't bat an eyelid about periods, body hair or anything normal women go through. He takes me any which way I come, hairy or smooth. He won't sit and wait for me to shave if he wants to show me some affection!

'Hairy McLary from Donaldson's Dairy!' shouted one of the kids from my year.

'Yeah, so what?' I called back, full of bravado, but hating

my nickname all the same. I looked down at my legs, which were swathed in thick winter tights, and saw the hairs poking through the weave.

'Just ignore them, Stace. They're not worth it,' my friend would say, every time I was referred to as the small black dog character from a well-known children's book.

I'd shrug but it hurt, probably because I felt ugly. I felt like a man. I couldn't wait to shave. I begged Mum for a razor. She refused, and made me wait until I was older before she let me wax.

There's only one word for waxing: excruciating. Awful. I couldn't believe the pain women willingly put themselves through. It put me off waxing for life.

After that I had to steal Mum's razors because I couldn't bear another trip to the waxer. For my last two years of secondary school I was shaving in secret because the boys were like 'Ugh, shave your legs!' That proved it wasn't just girls who were conditioned to find their natural hair repulsive: it affected boys and their perceptions of girls and women too.

As an adult, I've taken control. It's my body, I can decide to shave it or not. I just decided not to care what other people think. It works! I don't have time in my life to worry about whether someone is judging my hairy legs or not. If they are, I think they must have a very sad existence. I feel the same about online trolls. When I had that MASSIVE backlash on *Loose Women* about my body hair, I had loads of personal abuse thrown at me. Honestly, you'd have thought I'd committed a crime by sporting a bit of leg hair.

'Why are you so lazy?'

'Why can't you be bothered? It's disgusting and dirty.'

Would a man be called 'lazy' for not shaving his legs? *No!* It'd be ridiculous! (Unless, of course, he was about to do the Tour de France. I'm guessing long, wavy leg hairs are a serious impediment in terms of aerodynamics.) It's important we keep asking questions about everything we do. Am I shaving for myself or because people will disapprove if I don't? Thinking like that helps me to make clearer decisions.

Having hair doesn't make me any less of a woman. Do I care if twenty people I don't know make comments, or do I care more about what my partner, best friend or family thinks? I'd recommend training your brain to work in the same way, looking at who this really affects, and whether you care about those people and their opinions. It's a healthy mind habit, questioning what's important and looking at your decisions from a rational perspective.

Let's face it, shaving is a chore. Every woman I've ever spoken to about it will concede that point. It's a nightmare, to be frank. Expensive. Prone to unsightly shaving rash. And the grow-back is pure itch. For me, anyway.

If you want to shave, then shave. If you can't be bothered, and find you're spending the next week picking scratchy skin off your legs, then don't. Seriously, in-growing hairs are my kryptonite. It's about not getting caught up on how society wants us to behave. Let's make our decisions for our own reasons. I'm breaking the cycle. I'm saying it's okay to let it all hang out. It's natural. It should be *normal*. Shaving is not a necessity. It's not more hygienic (in fact, the reverse for lady gardens: the hair there is protective, stopping bacteria and pathogens from reaching our lady bits, and, even better, trapping pheromones, which produce arousal in prospective partners).

And, for your information, the bush is back. The 1970s rule again when it comes to body hair – and thank frickin' goodness for that! We can all let our pubes waft, knowing that we're totally on-brand, and future forward. Wa-hoo!

A nurse told me about the benefits of keeping my down-there hair unshaved just after I'd given birth to Zach. It was a revelation. It made me ask what shaving could do for me that healthy self-esteem, plus acceptance of myself and the natural workings of my incredible body couldn't. Answer: nothing! Nowadays, my sons revel in my hairy arms and legs. They call me 'Fuzzy', and it makes them giggle every time. I love that because I know I'm accepting that my hair is part of what makes me *me*. It's part of my happy body.

I strongly suggest you question your decision to depil-ate. Ask yourself, What's *my* happy? Shaving may make you feel sexier. It may just be a chore you resent. Perhaps it's time to look at the whole process objectively and decide if it still works for you. I'm not saying never shave anything ever again (unless you want to) but surely it's time to get your mind aligned with your body and ask, Does this work for me?

I've accepted my Hairy McLary badge. These days, I wear it – and my body hair – with pride.

Your body is your own. Don't let anyone tell you that you *have* to shave, but if you *want* to, it's your choice too. Let's celebrate our differences, our natural womanly bodies, and all that comes with them, including sexy fuzz!

STAY POSITIVE

The good news is that healthy mind habits can be learnt and, like any other new discipline, they need a bit of patience and trial-and-error along the way. Training your brain to look at the positives about you, your body and your life is vital to self-care and happiness. Every time a negative thought pops up, try to catch it, question it, and see it for what it is: just a thought.

Look at what triggers negative thoughts in your life. Perhaps it's seeing other people who seem to have 'better' bodies and lives.

Perhaps it's being in a relationship that doesn't feel right, or a career that feels only so-so. Check in with yourself. Keep turning those thoughts positive and get back in the driving seat.

CHAPTER 12

Finding Your True Self

Growing up, for me, was all about discovering who I really am, as opposed to who society, family or friends wanted me to be. The older I've got, the more confident I've become in following my heart and doing things my way. That's what finding my true self means to me – it's about being real, being me, and accepting myself for who I am, and also for who I'm not! It's about trying on the concept of self-love or, at the very least, self-acceptance and seeing if it fits. It's about appreciating who I am, what makes me happy and sad, and how I want to live this one precious life.

People say to me all the time, 'Never change, stay who you are,' which I find really weird. How could I possibly be anyone else, even if I tried? I'm in my most comfortable state of being because I'm just being me. I'm a terrible liar, and a worse actress, so I'd really struggle to be anything other than the weirdo I am. How would I change? Beats me. I think of it as my state of neutral. I know who I am, and I know what I know. I find it impossible to hide anything that's going on in my head.

No career in the diplomatic corps, then.

I really feel for people who have to put on a front – it must be exhausting.

I've watched actors who immerse themselves in a role, and I wonder if it's hard knowing where the character ends and they start.

I'm lucky. I've made a career of being myself. Alongside that, I'm always questioning myself. Where do I stand on this? Where does my compassion lie in that situation? It's good to check in with my values and, through my work on *Loose Women*, I'm learning more about myself and the world all the time. I hear someone else's opinion on something I've always thought otherwise about, and the clarity of their argument can enhance my understanding so that I change my mind. There's nothing wrong with changing your stance: it's a way of becoming more authentic – true to yourself and your values. When I'm prepared to be flexible and open-minded about an issue, I can check in with my values and line up my feelings with what's true for me. It may not be the same for you. Perhaps you are very clear about your values, and, if so, great!

I was brought up with a clear moral compass. My parents told me to do the right thing in each situation, be kind to people even if they'd upset me, and try to imagine what others might be going through if they're acting crazy or depressed. Those ideals run through everything I do, even when I feel conflicted – as I do on *Loose Women* all the time. We can have a meeting on a particular topic and I'll go in thinking I know exactly how I feel about it. By the time we've finished, Janet has spoken so eloquently or Jane has produced such convincing research that I totally change my mind. I love it when that happens!

My opinions may change but I'm still me. I'm the same girl who bunked off school and made silly jokes at the teacher's expense. I'm the same person who stood in front of the *X Factor* judges or who hung out in the rainforest. I'm just a human, like everyone else, and I'm most authentically 'me' when I'm being silly. I do things to make people laugh because I've always enjoyed making people happy. I've always really wanted people to like me, which might sound a bit sad, but it means I'm kinder to others as a result, which is good. I deal with the stresses – Motherload, Mum Guilt to name but two – that are an inevitable part of everyday life by making a fool of myself.

The classic example of this was when I launched into my crab impression on an Australian beach for Joe. We were right at the start of our relationship, and I'd gone over to surprise him. So what did I do? I decided to show the man I fancied my side-waddle. What a weirdo! Thank goodness I don't worry about looking like an idiot. In that moment, I was totally myself, totally happy, and it felt amazing. Actually, I was thinking as I was doing it, I do such a good crab impression! I'm really good at this …

I can also do a 'thumbs-up' with my big toe. Try it! It's harder than you think. I wave it in people's faces, especially my dad's, because it really winds him up. I love it. Talk about being in touch with my inner child, I don't think I ever became an outer adult! But I love making myself belly-laugh doing silly stuff, and when I'm doing it I feel totally at ease. When I'm in a good headspace I can have fun with my children, be present for Joe and really make the best, most comfortable decisions for us as a family. When I'm being completely me, the people around me relax and become more themselves. Perhaps by being real, we give permission to others to be themselves as well.

Every part of us reflects who we are and who we want to be, from our clothing to our hairstyles, the way we speak and behave. Sometimes it takes a bit of courage to wear what feels right, or say the things that are true for us. I don't always agree with some of the decisions my friends make, and I *could* just go along with them to keep the peace – but it wouldn't feel right. I'd feel I was lying to them if I didn't say what I think. They know I have their best interests at heart, which leaves me free to be honest because they know it's coming from a good place.

For most of us, our lives revolve around kids, school, work, money, relationships and, if we're lucky, a social life. When being an adult gets too much for me, I often revert to behaving like a ten-year-old to try to lighten a situation. I do it without thinking, but if you don't slip so easily into a playful mindset, there are ways to accomplish it. Looking at the silly side of a situation helps, as does remembering we are tiny specks on a small planet in the middle of a vast universe. When responsibilities seem heavy, I try to remember that I'm just one of seven billion people on this planet. That makes my problems seem insignificant, and helps me get my head back into a good place. Try it! It really works!

I've never worried about standing out, or being different, because I was so different from others as a child. I had to show my true colours from an early age. It can often be easier to follow the herd, or try to fit in, but how does that serve me? It can be hard to do things that go against the stream, but if we don't, what is the cost to ourselves in terms of our happiness? This is where my own core values come in.

I learnt so much from my parents about considering others and doing the right thing that I've developed some ethics of my own. Caring for my sons is at the heart of them, as is having purpose in life. I need something to get up for each morning and I have my boys and my work. My true happiness comes from shining my own light on my life, and taking full responsibility for my family's and my welfare.

I attracted a huge backlash online against my choice to take Zachary and Leighton out of mainstream schooling to be home-schooled. It was one of the hardest decisions I've made as a parent, and it took a year for me to pluck up the courage to say, 'I'm going for it.'

I was adamant that home-schooling offered the best environment for my boys, yet I recognized that school means children work on social interaction and relationship groups alongside the curriculum. I also felt conflicted because I am generally against private education, which you pay for.

I felt strongly that my eldest, Zach, was not built for the school system, and I saw him getting lost in it. He was quite disruptive in class because he wanted to know every single detail about each subject they were learning. When he was studying the Egyptians, he kept asking where they came from, who made Egypt, what is Palestine and so on. I know he didn't make it easy for his teachers, who had thirty pupils to engage so didn't have the time or resources to concentrate on one child. They had to keep saying, 'Zach, be quiet so we can finish the lesson.'

From that he took the idea that his questions were stupid. He felt he was being told off all the time, and his personality started to change. He began to lack confidence in himself, whereas before he had been a bright, inquisitive kid. I took him out of school before he lost his 'happy' altogether.

After lots of back and forth at the school, and lots of conversations with my parents and Zach's teachers, I decided to put the idea of home-schooling to him. I wanted to know if he felt that school was taking him in the direction he wanted to go. He was nine so the conversation was limited. He agreed that he wasn't getting on well at school and wanted to try different options so I floated the idea of learning at home. He responded reasonably well to the suggestion, but it took many more conversations to get his head around what it meant. Eventually, we all, but mostly Zach, felt home-schooling was the answer for him.

Leighton was in the nursery at the time. He could have stayed at school but he really wanted to be at home with

Zachary. I thought he should have the same style of schooling as his brother until he decides he wants to go to school, hopefully at an age when it's easy to slot into the state system. So far, Zach has adjusted really well. He isn't necessarily getting a better education, but he was struggling at school and now he isn't.

I've always felt that my curiosity and wonder at the world were brilliant tools. I can generally find something to marvel at even in the most unpromising situations. I could be sitting in pig poo, and I'd still be saying, 'Oh, isn't this nice? I'm so glad we did this.' I can be ridiculously positive, but life is more fun that way. It's my comfortable stance.

When Zach had homework, I would always expand it, research around it to find new, interesting things to wonder at. One of the nicest things we discovered was proof, in the story of the white moth that went black, that we are continually evolving. The Peppered Moth was in abundance before the Industrial Revolution, and could be either white or black. Within three years of industrial production beginning, scientists noticed the population of white moths had shrunk, while the black were prevalent. The species was excellent at camouflage so they'd evolved to fit in with their environment, which was dark with soot and smoke. Nothing, including your mindset, continues to stay the same.

Seeing Zach's wonder at the natural world around him being drained from him at school helped me to decide to home-school him. I wanted him to retain that interest in the world, to see his questions and the search for answers as a gift.

I have so much respect and admiration for teachers. I don't blame Zach's school at all. I saw loads of children flourishing there. We're all different, and I strongly believe one form of education does not fit us all.

Zach and Leighton now have a tutor once a week, and the rest of the week they have work sessions on what they've learnt. Then they are free to choose whichever subjects they want to learn about. We go to museums, the park, the Apple store, which offers free coding classes … The world is their oyster, and it came about because I had to look at what was working for them. My boys returned to their spirited selves, and I learnt to let go of other people's opinions because I'd made the right decision for us as a family.

Doing things our own way can be scary, yet it's vital we do that if we're going to be happily imperfect. It takes courage to be honest about who we are, especially if it goes against cultural or religious values. It can feel isolating at first, until we find kindred spirits.

Taking my boys out of school was terrifying, anxiety-inducing, but ultimately empowering. If I offer them any advice about how to do well in life, and discover what's important, it's never related to Pythagorus' Theorem. It's always about being true to yourself, even if that means taking the harder route, perhaps not fitting in with the group, taking the less lucrative job or breaking free from people who limit you or want to see you fail. In doing what I did, I taught the boys that they, too, can swim against the tide if they need to. They don't have to be the same as everyone else. We can evolve and change as circumstances dictate.

Finding out who we are and what works for us is vital to our wellbeing and our deep-down happiness. Get to know the inner 'you', the truthful version, even if that means accepting some uncomfortable things about yourself. None of us is all good, all kind and lovely – we'd be robots if we were. We're human, and humans make mistakes, get cross, do the wrong thing sometimes and fail regularly. All of this is okay because it's who we are. If you can accept the things that are not so nice about you then no one can say anything to you that you don't already know. And sometimes we have to say, 'Yes, I'm a bit flaky,' or 'No, I just don't feel like it and I know I sound selfish.' We all have a shadow side, which needs to be recognized and accepted before it can change.

Speaking your mind, wearing what feels right, acting in ways that don't fit in with what everyone else is doing are all inspiringly, ball-bustingly brave, and you owe it to yourself to live your best, most true-to-you life, even if it means sticking out a bit. We are all multi-dimensional, and what fits you might not fit someone else. Why do we expect people to fit into the same mould?

Be proud of who you are. Try not to worry about what other people think of you. Appreciate that they, too, are trying to live their best, most real lives, and consider keeping judgement at bay.

Looking at other people's viewpoints can be illuminating and inspiring. Are they acting from their true selves? If not, then why not? What's holding them back? I hope people are kind enough to ask the same questions of me if I'm acting wonky or making mistakes. Some days I can work a room and feel like Superwoman. On others I can stumble over my words and forget everyone's names. Some days I can be witty and gregarious, and on others I can't think what to say.

That's life. That's what being human is all about: messing up at one minute, then being stunning at the next.

Only you can know what truly floats your boat, what makes you *you*. By making decisions based on that knowledge, you get to live your most true life.

STAY POSITIVE

Doing things your own way is a sure-fire means to becoming happily imperfect. Be bold.

Take your dreams seriously. Uncover the amazing person you are, and find your happy in your way. Don't be afraid to show your true colours – even if it means upsetting a few people. Living in fear of judgement is living a half-life. Act from the heart. How can you be more true to yourself right now?

The Japanese word *ikigai* translates as 'reason for being' or 'purpose'. It's about looking at the things in life that give you purpose and meaning. *Ikigai* is individual to each and every person on the planet, and is a reflection of our inner selves.

Finding your *ikigai* is about looking at your core values, what you like to do and what you're good at. Look at your passions. See where they lead you, because that's where your life purpose lies. Follow your bliss, even if it means stepping away from the herd.

At first, you may struggle or fail. You may lack motivation. Pick yourself up, dust off your values and beliefs, and keep going. There is a crock of gold at the end of this rainbow.

CHAPTER 13

The Hype

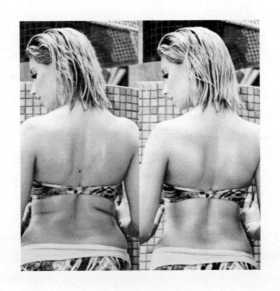

The 'gram. Twitter. Facebook. LinkedIn. Google +. Tumblr. Snapchat. Pinterest. YouTube. Vimeo. Chances are you're on at least one of the big sharing platforms.

Never have our lives been so transparent – or so curated. I love connecting with people on social media. It's such a great feeling to chat to people I'd probably never meet in real life because our paths wouldn't cross. I have a right laugh on Twitter and Instagram, and get to share pictures from my everyday life – its ups and downs – and draw on followers and fans for support. There's so much good to be had from engaging with these platforms … as long as I remember that none of it is real, and that I should take it all lightly. There has never been another time in human history when we've been able to reach out to as many people as we can today, engaging with others across the globe, and have access to so much information.

It's an amazing, magical thing, but social media has its dark side.

For me, that's being bombarded with all those images of 'perfect' lives. You know the ones I mean. They're the yoga-guru, green-smoothie-guzzling, perfect-skin, perfect-life, sunset-wielding people, who present me with everything my life isn't. It's all got a bit out of hand, and I think we're reaching a backlash. It's about time. Honestly, if I see another yoga-postured beauty I may vomit.

To be fair, these images aren't just propagated on social media: newspapers and magazines are just as guilty. It's everywhere: on billboards, on our newsfeeds and on our sharing platforms. We're surrounded by a sea of information, opinion and advertising that has become a tsunami of perfection.

Well, I want to join the likes of Celeste Barber, whom I mentioned earlier, and counter-attack the hype. I want to acknowledge that we're all just human beings: we all have bad breath in the morning or pick off bits of flaky skin (unless that's just me). We're all capable of great things, and not-so-great things, and we all have our quirks. In fact, those are the bits that make us unique and special.

Just having a quick scroll as I write this, I can see that, apparently, there's so much more I could be doing to make my life better (who knew?). Apparently, I could be doing better at *everything*. There you go! I thought I was doing a great job at life until all those hacks came along. Within five minutes of looking through a few bloggers, vloggers and Instagrammers my head is already asking: 'Am I pretty enough? Am I working out enough, and in the right way? Am I eating the right foods? Should I be vegan? Paleo?

Gluten-free? Should my parenting look like this? Or that? What are my relationship goals? Do I do enough to keep Joe's and my relationship alive?'

Oh dear.

A billion people out there are sharing images of perfection, telling us how to do stuff 'properly'. They weren't there twenty years ago, so why now? I wonder if we've all stopped following our instincts, and instead follow Instagram. We're being pulled into a fantasy world where everyone is flawless, their homes and lives are enviable.

Now, there's nothing wrong with a little envy. Most of us push ourselves forward in life because we like the look of that shiny car, or we want an extra bedroom at home or nicer holidays. It's part of the human condition to want what others have and not feel left behind. But we've gone too far. Who isn't bogged down in this stuff?

I'm pretty sure that being inundated with unhealthy expectations for our lives is destructive to our sense of self. It must be. If we are constantly comparing ourselves to others in terms of what they have, what they look like, how successful they are, there's going to be a moment when we look at our own selves and lives and think, I'm not good enough, and I'm never going to be good enough. Aaaargh!

There is no such thing as normal, perfect or regular. Instead, there are people, circumstances and places. Everyone is unique and every situation is different. For example, I'm obsessed with getting my health checked out and I know my blood pressure is low, but my GP says, 'It isn't low, it's normal for you.' That's my 'normal'. Also, my hair is extremely thick, but that's my normal too. My boobs are ginormous, and that's my normal. Joe and I are trying to get pregnant and I know that my cycle doesn't fit with the 'normal' range and that's okay as well. Neither I nor my siblings were born with wisdom teeth, and that's our normal. I don't fit the mould, and I'm betting you don't either.

I remember scrolling through Instagram a couple of years ago, thinking, Oh, my gosh, my pictures don't look anything like these. My flabby bits were hanging out, while everyone else was perfect, taut and smooth. It made me question who I was following and why I was following them. But even the friends I've known all my life appeared marginally different, or 'better', than their true selves. From that moment, I knew I had to become more clued-up with the world of social media. I realized it's mostly a photo shoot, the same as any magazine would use, and it's definitely not real life.

I spoke to my friends who are on social media, and discovered there was a multitude of apps and settings, and even equipment that people were using to achieve those perfect pictures. Facetune is an app that allows you to press a button which automatically retouches skin, makes your eye whites whiter, and even reduces the appearance of wrinkles or fine lines. When I learnt that, my first thought was, Why are we doing this? Why are we all trying to look the same? I did give it a go on one of my pictures, but I just couldn't get my head around the fact that the app didn't discriminate between wrinkles and smile lines. I lost my facial character, and looked like a waxwork. I knew then that such apps were not for me, though I'm not judging anyone for using them.

We all aspire to be a bit more glamorous than perhaps we are, and there's nothing wrong with that. I also saw I could make a difference by showing the real 'me' in contrast to that slew of perfection. I won't airbrush or Photoshop my image because I don't want the people who follow me to feel like I did as I looked through my newsfeed that day. I'm in the public eye and I feel I have a responsibility not to impact people's lives in a negative way. I want to say to my followers that of course it's okay to be you, however that you-ness presents itself, even though it flies in the face of everything we're told: so much out there begs to differ.

There are people who say that the next generation will be canny enough to see through the masks, sort out what's real and what's not. I hope that's true, but I believe that isn't enough. We can't deny that the standards set by such apps aren't a massive problem for the way young people perceive themselves. When we expose people to images of airbrushed perfection across the media and in advertising, we know they suffer low self-esteem, depression and eating disorders as a result. A 2018 study carried out by a team of economists at Sheffield University found that children who spent more time on social media were less happy: it impacted their feelings about their appearance and life. This is crazy. Should social media carry a health warning?

We are in danger of creating an age of anxiety. It's hard enough for us adults to untangle what's real and what's a photo shoot, let alone for our children. Mental health is a big issue, and I'm not suggesting that social media is the only cause of unhappiness, but I do wonder how damaging it can be to look at ourselves, our bodies and our lives and believe that none of them is up to scratch.

It seems to me that not enough people are saying reality *is* good enough, so I'm going to spell it out. You are perfectly imperfect, unique and beautiful *however* you look. Shocking or exhilarating?

None of us escapes the pressure to be perfect, and celebs can be the worst for showing us their glitzy lives and unachievable blow-dries, yet none of us gets to exist without a few weird and wonderful bits on our bodies. Let's celebrate them. Let's ignore what we're being told. To me, being imperfect means, by definition, we don't have movie-set backgrounds to our lives, and we don't have perfectly smooth skin or sleek hair.

I have a confession. I don't know if you've heard of Weebles? Perhaps you're too young, but they were a roly-poly egg-shaped toy from the 1970s that wobbled everywhere. I feel like one most days because I have size four feet yet I'm five foot seven inches tall. Basically, I need way more foot surface to be properly stable. Most of the time, I feel as if I career about, just like a Weeble, and I can assure you that this does not feel glamorous. I'm telling you this because I could present my life as easier than it is, but I can't bring myself to do that. It would feel like I was betraying the trust my loyal followers have in me. I want to stand for good old-fashioned honesty. I want to portray my life as it really is, and sometimes it's amazing and the four of us are flying off to LA so I can work, then the next day I'm clearing out the cat-litter tray with my false eyelashes hanging off my cheeks because I slept in them the night before.

I'm all about celebrating the stuff that isn't airbrushed.

Social media is brilliant for connecting with people. I can share stuff with my family and friends that they wouldn't get to see otherwise. I can have an opinion, have a voice, and enjoy seeing what others are up to. That's the warm, fuzzy side of it. We have to be savvy, though. We have to engage with this tool in the full knowledge that people are being paid to reflect certain lifestyles, that they are being paid to be 'influencers', and that we'll probably never be as pretty or rich or skinny as them – and why would we bother? It's totally fine not to be!

You may say it's easy for me to show off my wobbly bits or discuss my #lifefails. I have a huge support system online and in real life. I have incredibly loyal followers who have got my back, who support me when I need it, and all that is true. Only recently I called out *Now* magazine for printing a front-page picture of me, calling me 'boring', 'desperate' and 'cheap'. I tweeted that it was the meanest thing I'd seen. That stuff, cobbled together from social-media comments about me, is, frankly, sinister.

The magazine was basically saying that my sense of body confidence was boring, and people are getting sick of it. What kind of message is that to the young women who may read that story? How close does it come to bullying, and how can we change the climate of abuse online? To me, it was a classic example of tearing women down for liking their imperfect bodies. How the hell can young women, or men, feel secure in themselves and their bodies if they read stuff like that? *Now* magazine, along with every other media outlet, has a huge responsibility to its readers, a responsibility that stories like that abuse.

I'm lucky. I had loads of support when I tweeted my reaction to the story, but it shouldn't have been written in the first place. It's time for the tide to turn, for us to question everything we read. Does that sit with my values? Does it feel okay? And if it doesn't? We reject it. We unfollow. We mute. We click to sign out. There are certain people I've decided to unfollow because I can't look at their feeds any more. I need some light relief.

I follow my fans because I'd rather fill my newsfeed with their posts rather than waste any more time on brands. I don't follow many influencers any more either. I follow my friends, the people and brands I work with (and I choose those because I really like them, and feel I can be myself when I work with them).

I think being myself (not some Stepford Wife) is all I can do on a personal level. I can't have a go at someone because they look perfect. There's nothing wrong with looking amazing. I'm hardly going to say, 'Can you look a bit less pretty, please?' but I do think there should be space for everybody to be themselves and, most importantly, to be true to themselves.

I've posted pictures of Joe and me looking glamorous on nights out or at awards parties. That's fine. Just so long as you know that an hour before the photo was taken I was wrestling with my hair curlers while de-fleaing the cat, and shouting at my sons to keep the noise down as they played a particularly animated game of Fortnite.

We all choose the most flattering shots to represent ourselves and our lives. There's nothing wrong in that either, as long as we remember we're all humans, with human problems, weird bodies and messy lives. This is reality, not the selfie we're sharing because people will think we're cool or will like us more.

I hope I have a social conscience, which I apply on my social media by trying not to just post the good stuff. I think it stems from the values I was taught – try not to upset anyone – but also from having children. I don't want them to feel inadequate because their lives don't resemble the ones they see online.

Zachary asked me recently: 'Mummy, when am I going to grow my own six-pack?'

'*Whaaaat?* Why are you asking me this?' I was totally shocked.

'I want to look like a super-hero,' he said, like it was the most natural ambition in the world.

I had to explain to him that, in order to possess a six-pack, the person has to make big changes to their diet and do lots of exercise. I had to explain that six-packs don't grow, they're a product of hard work and a strict regime.

But why even ask that question at the age of ten? He's been conditioned to believe that's how men look. All his super-heroes have big muscular bodies, so he believes acquiring one is a life goal.

And nothing out there contradicts this information. There's nothing to tell our kids that having a ripped body isn't the norm, and that there's room to be beautiful, appreciated and loved, whatever we look like. Where's the diversity? Where's the love for humankind in all its shapes and forms?

I'm happy as I am because I ignore a lot of the gloss that gets posted, except when I feel the need to say, 'No, this isn't acceptable.'

For me, it's about looking inside myself and making sure I'm happy with who I am. If I fully accept myself, muffin tops and all, I can happily engage with social media or marketing, because I know who I am and what I stand for.

I truly believe that everyone is a perfect version of themselves. As you know, when I was growing up, I had the thickest bushy eyebrows, which were a trauma for me, but now fat brows are all the rage. If you give it a few years, everything you worry about will probably become something everyone loves!

Essentially, I want my sons to know what's real – and what isn't. I want them to fully love themselves as they are, not for the amount of 'likes' they receive. They are growing up in a world of social media, they've never known any different, and yet, for most of us, those Instagram-perfect lives are completely unachievable. Where does that leave my boys? Will they see it for what it is, a representation of a life rather than reality, or will they worry about fitting the current ideals, the images of perfection they will be bombarded with? I'm an adult and I still get hurt by nasty comments online – it's impossible not to. How much more of an effect will it have on my boys when the lines are so blurred between fact and fiction?

We're all vulnerable.

No, you won't look like the woman in the chocolate ad, however hard you try, because only she looks like her, and she's a model.

No, you won't look like the man with muscles and a perfect stubbly chin when you buy the razors he's advertising, because only he looks like him, and he's a friggin' model too.

I will have to keep reminding them, and myself, that even if someone says something negative about us publicly, we're still okay, and we're still amazing people who love each other.

This chapter is my call to action. Let's all start questioning every magazine article that puts women down for being normal – for having cellulite or gaining a few pounds (or losing them). Let's all tune out the stuff online and in the media that makes us feel inadequate. I can't stress this enough: you are beautiful as you are. Your life is probably messy, chaotic, funny, heartbreaking, silly, ridiculous and amazing – just like mine – and that's how it's meant to be.

Let's all set our own standards. Let's focus on being the best 'me' we can be, regardless of what society says. Let's recognize it's pretty much all total c**p – and it's fine to be just okay. In fact, it's amazing to be okay.

Let's agree not to give ourselves a hard time for not achieving unachievable goals of perfection. Next time you're cracking open a packet of Digestives instead of whizzing up a green smoothie, cut the life guilt and revel in the moment. Enjoy!

STAY POSITIVE

Is it time for a digital detox?

Don't be afraid not to be a part of social media. You don't have to be on Facebook, Instagram or Twitter. You really don't. If it's having a detrimental effect on you, try switching off your devices for a day or two. Putting my phone down gives me a chance to live my life in the way I would live it without the worry of social media. I can step back from that world, even though I love connecting with people, and give myself a psychological breather. The images of perfection are way less powerful when I'm connected to my real life.

Most of us spend far too much time looking at screens. We all know it has an effect on our sleep patterns, but it also disconnects us from what's actually going on in our lives. It isn't just about how social media continually invites us to make comparisons with each other: it's also about how it takes us away from the life that's around us.

CHAPTER 14

Rose-tinted Goggles

Life is blimmin' serious. There are so many twists and turns. We've got to decide where to live, what kind of schooling we want, whether to get married, whether to have children, whether to move up in our careers.

Not taking any of that too seriously is my tonic. You know how people have a glass of wine to relax when they get home? Well, I have to do something silly. Instead of a glass of wine (I don't really drink) I might wrestle with Joe or scare my kids. Joe and I play a game. He waits until I'm walking up the stairs, then pounces, trying to grab my leg. I know it sounds crazy, but it's so creepy it makes me laugh hysterically. Once he's managed to grab me, he won't let go and I'll generally find myself rolling around on the stairs, trying to escape his clutches. Don't ask me why I like it. It sounds completely bonkers, but if I'm feeling any stress when I get in from work, it vanishes because we're laughing so much.

As you'll have guessed, Joe and I share a really childish sense of humour, but that isn't the only way we have learnt to unwind and reconnect as a family.

Being in the 'now' is the key to not taking life too seriously. It's when I'm totally in the moment, not thinking about the past or the future, just what's going on right now in my world. It's so easy to project ahead, when I'm worrying about my mortgage or a big workload that's coming my way. Let's face it, most of us spend half our lives worrying about what happened in the past or what will happen in the future. Yet once I realize I'm not living in the present it can be so simple to bring myself back. All it takes is a moment to savour what's happening right now. For me, that's anticipation of my lunch, which my mum is helping me prepare, while one of the cats strokes its tail against my leg. I'm safe, warm and about to eat, and life slips back under my rose-tinted goggles when I appreciate just how lucky I am to have food on the table and a roof over my head.

It's also about finding those moments when I can escape from the world, get away from it all, and just 'be'. During the last eclipse, the kids and I lay in the garden together and stared at the sky. It was so hot. The feel of the night air on our skin was magical, and so was letting the sky fill our eyes. Those moments when nothing else is going on in your head, when you allow yourself just to exist, are so precious.

Ironically, we didn't actually see anything. We just stared up at the sky for ages and wondered at the sheer enormity of the galaxy. It was like a small holiday from life, yet it was about going deeper into life at the same time. So powerful.

Sometimes life is so busy and full-on for all of us. We're told to think of the future, pay our mortgages, consider how we'll fund our old age or our children's college course. At that moment, though, it wasn't necessary for me to think or feel anything other than being in the present, just being. For a short time, it felt like the world had stopped, and all the things I worry or panic about became irrelevant. My boys were happy. They were enjoying the lack of hustle and bustle. They were enjoying being calm and still, peaceful together, which doesn't happen often, believe me! They had the space and time to ask the sorts of questions about the universe, the stars and the sky that neither Joe nor I had the answers to.

None of us was regretting the past or thinking about the next thing or the next day. We were experiencing the present, in a neutral state of happiness. It was an incredibly easy yet profound shift into a new headspace.

Even in the trickiest situations it can be possible to surrender to the moment, live in the now. When my brother Matt and I decided to take the children to see the turtles on a Greek beach, Matt was convinced it was fine to drive onto a sandy path to get closer to them. We found out pretty soon that we had completely the wrong car for that – a small Fiesta, not a 4x4. The car stopped moving and we saw it was about a metre deep in sand. I didn't have any phone battery, while Matt's was in the red zone. We called the motor rescue people, and Matt somehow managed to let them know where we were.

Then the sun literally dropped out of the sky, and within

minutes it was pitch-black. Once we knew someone was aware of where we were, we were laughing. We waited on that beach for hours. I looked up at the sky, and it was a blanket of stars. There was no light anywhere and they were so clear – there were millions of them. Every minute there were shooting stars. We lay on the beach and stared at the sky, totally unaware that we were being eaten alive by sand flies.

It taught me there's beauty everywhere if we look for it.

In our everyday lives it's hard to find that time and space, and it doesn't happen often, but when it does, it can change how we feel in an instant. It also serves to remind us that we should lighten up, look at life less seriously, because there's a huge universe out there and we're an infinitesimally tiny part of it. That thought helps me to see my problems or fears in a new light. They seem less significant, somehow.

It doesn't always have to be a meaningful connection with nature that springs me back into the present. It can be something fun that makes me giggle, and probably something spontaneous that I wasn't expecting. For example, my little brother Joshua will come over, and I'll ask him to help Zachary put my clothes away while I make lunch. A few minutes later, he'll come down wearing them all – every top, every jacket and pair of trousers or skirt. Everything. The first time he did it, I just stared at him for a moment, and then we both burst out laughing. For the rest of the day I couldn't stop giggling as the image of him dressed in all my clothes kept flashing in my mind. Things like that serve to take me out of whatever I was worried about or working on, and just enjoy a moment of hilarity. I love it when that happens.

It's also about cultivating the art of not being too fussed if things happen, or don't happen. For example, if I don't fancy going out, I don't go out. I don't stress. It's not worth thinking about. I'd rather sit at home, in my pyjamas and unicorn slippers, than have a night out. So, if I'd rather do that, why not just do it?

I know I'm lucky that I can switch off my brain at times and just enjoy the moment. Not all of us can, due to mental-health issues, such as depression. It can be much harder to put aside negative thoughts and experience a moment, so this chapter may be challenging for people who have experienced mental ill health. It isn't always possible to put on a pair of rose-tinted goggles and appreciate the world from a happy place. I know people who have suffered from depression, as I do with anxiety, and when they're going through those difficult times it's virtually impossible to step outside the circling thoughts and into the present. I know that mindfulness can be a brilliant tool for people who are struggling, and I guess this is my version of it, but it may not work for everyone. I just want to share what works for me in the hope it might work for you too.

The way we're built chemically makes a massive difference to how we feel. In a lot of difficult situations I try to decide that I'd rather be happy than unhappy, and that isn't always easy. It takes presence of mind to step back from a situation and not react, and I don't always have that. There are certain times of the month when I don't have any control over my thoughts, when I cry at everything, feel totally insecure and hate the world. Hormones play a big part in that.

On the whole I'm definitely a glass-half-full person. My sister is the opposite. When we recount certain times in our lives round the dinner table, I'll say something like: 'Do you remember that time we went camping? It was *sooo* good. We got them stick-on nails. We made loads of friends.' Jemma will have been on the same trip but have a different memory: she'd describe it as 'that rubbish camping trip where we bought stick-on nails, and they fell off'.

She sees life differently yet she's no less happy than I am. She's just not saying, 'Wow, this is wonderful,' all the time, like I do. The world contains billions of people. None of us is the same (okay, identical twins may beg to differ), and we all have our ways of coping, none of which is more or less valid than others. Most of the time, I can laugh things off. I was born with that ability, and it's the way my chemical makeup is set. My sister wasn't born like that. She is more realistic, more likely to look at things as they are, rather than through those rosy goggles, and that's okay too. I think it's all on a spectrum of coping abilities. I wouldn't say that Jemma is any less happy with herself than I am, and we're totally different personalities.

My anxiety, though problematic, helps me love life way more. That's the flip side of it. My fear of losing the opportunity to be alive on this earth makes me think, Wow!, all the time. I just find everything amazing, brilliant, wonderful and exciting, because I never know when it's going to end. I want it all to last for ever.

There are downsides to that. It makes me quite naïve. My sister will get a vibe that tells her, 'This person is not a good person and they're not going to treat you right,' while I can't see that at all. I assume everyone is kind and has a good heart. Sometimes that can leave me in sticky situations. I have found myself being used in the past because I don't see the bad in people. I know I'm a sucker, that I trust people before they've proved to me that they're trustworthy, but I accept it because it's just how I am. Actually, most of the time I find out that people are good and can be trusted. Yay to the human race!

There are positives and negatives to everything. Every reaction has an equal and opposite reaction, as Newton's Third Law states. There is good and bad in everything. I view life through rose-tinted goggles. It's who I am, and who I choose to be.

Let's face it, we're all stressed. We live in a world where our targets are unachievable, living costs are enormous, and there's a lot of pressure to be 'better'. They say that stress is the biggest killer, and most of us can't change our circumstances, which makes it more important than ever not to take things too seriously.

Being able to go back to your childhood, and remember your inner child is so important. I remember my mum and dad being really stressed out when we were growing up.

They had three kids, a mortgage, and Dad was starting a company. Mum was the breadwinner. There was loads of pressure on them, but we still had moments where we would just be silly together. My dad would take the mickey out of us. We had a hamster, and my sister had a toy kitchen, and he would tell us he was cooking the hamster for dinner and put her in the toy oven. Those silly moments when he got to forget about the stresses of his work, and we got to enjoy our dad, were amazing. For me, it's about finding those moments when I'm mucking about with my boys or Joe, sharing silly times, and everything else fades away.

A positive mental attitude is helpful. It means I can turn pretty much any negative into a positive outcome, even if it just means changing the way I feel about something. For example, when *Now* magazine wrote that nasty stuff about me in 2018 calling me boring and cheap, I knew I had to speak out. I was really upset and could have hidden away, but I didn't. I used that feeling to challenge the prevailing attitudes towards women and their bodies by these magazines.

Hopefully, what happened to me will help change the way magazines write about women, celebrity or not, and that's a wonderful outcome from a horrible situation. There are some amazing new magazines out there such as *Happiful*, whose editorial stance is to shed light on young people's mental health and build self-esteem – not to pull us apart and criticise. We're all good enough and that's what's important to remember.

With my kids, even if I'm worried about something, or they're acting crazy, I make sure I turn it around and do something fun like building a den, often when I'm meant to be getting ready for work or a night out! As a single mum I could be the strict one, and they could see their dads as the fun ones, but it doesn't work like that for us. We're all basically idiots, having fun together as much as we can, and we love it.

When it comes to my appearance, I love making myself up differently every day, but I'm not precious about it: I don't feel any prettier or better as a person. I outed my friend Suze, the wig I bought to cover my ruined, over-bleached hair, on social media while giving her a bath. That's how seriously I *don't* take my looks.

We all know there are lots of things we *have* to take seriously – our homes, the wellbeing of our loved ones, our jobs – but I reckon we could all do with lightening up a bit, taking the load off, and living more in the process.

I'm learning to give less of a c**p what other people think of me. I've got an Essex Girl accent and a lazy eye that flickers when I'm nervous. I've had online trolls, newspapers being mean about some of the things I've worn, and paparazzi stalking me when I'm taking my kids to the park. I should be a nervous wreck because I care about what people think of me, but these days I'm taking it with a bigger pinch of salt than I ever have.

So, how is that even possible? I suffer from anxiety, I'm definitely a people-pleaser, and I work in the public eye so I attract lots of comments. It should be a recipe for disaster!

Again, it's because I try to focus on all the positives in any given situation. Nine times out of ten the comments and responses I receive from people, whether online or in real life, are nice. Yet I've found that the small minority of negative comments implant themselves in my brain. When I looked at it objectively, I realized that if I can allow those nasty comments to affect me I must be able to do the same with the nice ones and let them affect me in a positive way.

Now I mostly just reply to the positive messages, and I try to allow those to soak in, not the negative ones. I'm learning to trust the positives, to let them mean something to me, just as the horrible comments did.

Trusting that things will work out, and people are basically good, has helped me get where I am today because I'm open to new people and experiences. Saying that, I've needed help at times. I was at Euston station the other day. I only had my bank card, but I was busting for the toilet, and I needed exactly 40p (or 60p, I can't remember) in coins. I didn't have it. I got some cash out but by then I was desperate: I was holding my nunny and shouting, 'I don't have any change!' waving my £5 note. A woman came along and put the money in the machine, saying, 'Go, go!' So many people are kind, which always puts me in a positive frame of mind. I like focusing on the good bits because they make my life better.

Not giving a c**p about other people's opinions is a lot easier when I surround myself with people who love me, and who have my back, whether they be family or friends. Being nice to yourself is important because it means you can trust yourself to know that you're everything someone is saying you're not. If someone comments negatively and that really affects you, try to find that place inside yourself where you believe you're the opposite. Other people don't define you, or have the ability to tell you who you are. You can say, 'No, that's not who I am.'

Try to get your power back. Some people can take it away from us, perhaps with mean comments, and it's about being able to train yourself to override the effects of their disapproval with your own self-belief. Get yourself back to a place where you own your own power, and nobody else does.

No one has permission to make us feel bad. Self-belief and self-acceptance are the antidotes to other people's opinions. Stick to your guns. Believe in your ability to take back your own power. I try to live my best life – and part of that is learning, slowly but surely, not to give a c**p what anyone else thinks of me.

Finding perspective is really helpful. Now and then something happens and I feel angry or upset. I ask myself, 'Is it worth getting cross about this? Should I risk upsetting someone else if I get angry here? Is it worth upsetting them? Is this really important?' and, even, 'Is this my problem to deal with?' If the answer to any of those is 'No', I let it go. Simple as that. Finding a positive perspective gets easier with practice. I can't control what goes on in my life sometimes, but I can control my reactions to it.

Remember that most people are good. Most people don't want to upset me, so I can assume positive intent on their part. I honestly believe that many more people are nice than nasty, so let's treat them in that way, even if it means taking a risk on someone.

Do stuff that makes you laugh. Find your 'happy'. What works for me, might not work for you. I love mucking about with my kids, putting on silly voices, or wrestling with Joe. Your happy might be completely different. You might like putting on uplifting music, or watching funny films, or seeing friends who make you laugh.

It's also about leaving perfection behind. We're all perfectly imperfect: let's be happy about that and enjoy our weird, stupid, crazy bits. We've all got them, believe me!

Do whatever you need to do to minimize stress – perhaps you're into yoga or maybe meditation hits the spot. Go for it. If your diet needs to upgrade with more fruit and veg, now's the time. If negative news on the telly or in the newspapers is bringing you down, turn it off, or throw them away, and reset your fun dial. Hanging out with people who make me smile is always my default happy place.

When everything I'd ever dreamt of was at stake, when I was one step away from the final twenty-four of *The X Factor*, when my hopes, ambitions and desires were culminating in the climax of my life, I still couldn't stop myself being the class clown.

'What will you do if you don't get through?'

'This is my life. If I can't do this, I don't know what I'm going to do, although there's always Asda!'

That was my ridiculous take on the roller-coaster, life-changing, now-or-never, cataclysmically terrifying last few auditions to get through to the final. I was being interviewed, and despite all that pressure, I still couldn't help unleashing my inner idiot.

We all take life too seriously at times. We know it's important to learn how to de-stress and lighten up. I rely on my goofiness to see me through the stressful stuff, and, yay, it's always on hand!

Even at the most inconvenient times, it's possible to get into the now, to forget about the past or the future and to live totally in the present. How can you do that right now?

How can you find a moment of calm and beauty in your daily routine? Living in the moment is tricky in our fast-paced world but if we take the time to tune out, get back to the present, it can focus our hearts on what's really important. I'm slapping my rose-tinted goggles firmly on my face today. Why don't you give them a try? You never know what may happen if you take the lighter, easier route through your day.

STAY POSITIVE

Choose positivity – even if this feels too 'woo-woo' for you, even if life is a struggle each day. Try choosing to go with the one positive thought among the million negative ones.

Choose to trust that things will be okay, even if they look bleak. Open your eyes to the good that really does exist in your world, even if it's only tiny things right now. It's about training your brain again. If we keep choosing the positive over the swampy negatives, we may be able to accept parts of our life that feel tricky, and even help someone else to be happy with our own bright new outlook.

Daily life is filled with positives and negatives: I can choose how I react, whether I let the negative stuff in. I have a happier life because I can focus on what feels good.

CHAPTER 15

Blended Families

loved being part of a blended family. We had two Christmases, two birthdays, and two Hanukkahs every year. I'm also pretty sure that both of my parents tried to give us the best Christmas they could so they were in competition over the best presents, the biggest feast ...

The way I saw it, there were more people on our team. I learnt to see the newcomers as potential teammates rather than rivals, and that's my best advice to anyone in this situation. By embracing the changes, by looking at new people as more people on your side, you're always adding to your tribe.

So much of being in a blended or step-family set-up was beneficial. It worked on so many different levels, and it enhanced my relationships with both of my natural parents. That was a consequence I'd never expected. It was great having a completely objective parent: I could confide in one about the other without having to air my problem to both. I could share more with my parents than I would have done otherwise, and share different things with them rather than having to tell them the same things all the time.

My parents were amazing. It was entirely because of their unselfishness that we made the transition so successfully from our original family into a larger one. They had calmly told us about the end of their marriage and, in time, introduced Karen. From the start we all hung out together, which made things seem more 'normal' than if they had done things differently. We weren't at all unsettled by the changes.

In hindsight, Mum and Dad made our lives better as a result of their divorce. Our parents were happier separated than they had been when they were married. At the time, half of my classmates were going through their parents' divorce, and often it wasn't being dealt with very well. Seeing that, and realizing how lucky I was, made me more understanding of what other people were going through. It was a really positive lesson to learn.

Our blended family is brilliant. I love it. I love my stepmum Karen, and that she and my mum can be in the same room together – can even spend Christmas together. There's never been any animosity, and their friendship made the change as seamless as it could be in the circumstances. As a grown woman with children, and exes, of my own, I know how much they must have sacrificed emotionally to do that for us. Growing up, I realized our situation was unique. It must be so hard for families if a divorce isn't amicable. If there's ever the tiniest chance of having a peaceful relationship with your partner after a split, and children are involved, you've got to go for it.

My experience is such a contrast to how the media portrays broken or blended families. It's rare to come across positive depictions of joined-up families on adverts or in books. Most happy-ever-afters involve the classic man-meets-woman, they fall in love, have children and live happily ever after. We all know real life doesn't work that way at least half the time as half of marriages end.

I know how lucky I was as a child because, with my children, I can't have the same relationship with my exes or their partners as my parents had. My exes aren't my dad, and their partners aren't my step-mum, and everyone deals with things differently. It takes a lot to get rid of any animosity and to make it all about the children. Sometimes it's impossible in some families, my own included, and it's a great shame. Things can end badly despite our best efforts, and there's nothing you can do about it, even with the best intentions. That can be hard to accept. It's taken me a long time to accept that's the way it is for me, and we just have to live our lives as best we can, putting the boys first. It's impossible to force somebody to want to be a part of your life because you've got a child together: that person will decide if they want that or not. My divorce didn't work out the way my mum and dad's did and I have to accept that – people's ideologies are different.

Having come from a 'broken' family, and as a single mum to my two boys, I am passionate about unravelling the myths and truths of so-called broken homes. I refuse to believe what I'm told in the media about boys becoming criminals because no father was around in their childhood. Reports like that blame both separated parents: mothers for not doing a good enough job, and fathers for not being around and not caring enough. I don't accept that. If it were so, all boys raised by single mums or in unconventional set-ups would commit crime – and they don't.

We have to reject those stories. People raised outside societal norms can go on to lead productive, happy lives. They can become good people as much as anyone else. There are so many other factors at play: circumstance, chance, the people you meet, the wider environment you grow up in, the financial context, the expectations of those around you, and schooling, to name a few.

A million and one elements will determine a person's outcome. I do believe that if you work your hardest to become the best parent you can be, that is all you can ever do. I'll do whatever I can to provide for my sons and I let them know constantly how much they're loved. Even when I'm angry with them they always know I love them. I just try to teach them the moral values instilled in me by my parents: try to do the right thing, try to go down the right path, try to resist the temptation to do something that may feel like the easy way forward but could get you into lots of trouble. Even with two great, stable parents I was still a rebellious child: our children are born with their own personalities and are going to be their own people at the end of the day. We just have to try to mould them, and guide them in the right direction, but we all know that doesn't mean they'll listen.

I never listened to my parents. They'll sit with me today and say, 'Oh, we probably shouldn't have done this or that', and I say, 'What the hell!' My decisions to skive off and be naughty in class were mine: they were no reflection on my parents. At the end of the day, all seven of us siblings are decent human beings so they definitely did something right.

There is so much underlying pressure. We're told to worry about the decisions we're making because society tells us, 'Your family needs something else.' If we don't stay with one person for the rest of our life, then we probably won't be having the best life.

Luckily, I don't believe that.

There is lots of evidence that staying in unhappy relationships has a detrimental effect on people's lives. It's certainly not the be-all-and-end-all if your parents aren't together, or if you decide to split up from your relationship. Again, it's all about conditioning. Society tells us that the perfect family is made up of attractive parents with 2.4 children, a Volvo and a nice house, but that's not the reality for most of us. Not having that fairytale doesn't make us any less of a family. It doesn't mean we love each other any less. Your family can be anything you make it.

I know lots of people who have come out of foster care and built their own family with friends. It doesn't have to be biological parents, brothers or sisters. There are so many people in my life I consider family who aren't blood relations, and my parents were the same. As a child, I had 'uncles' and 'aunties' who weren't related to me: they were really close friends of my parents or grandparents, and I respected them as much as our actual relatives. They were there for us, they were part of our lives.

Even if a family breaks down, it doesn't change the fact that they are still your family.

You can keep the idea of family, even though you're not still together. My children have their dads' families and they have our family. They're not two separate things: they're part of the same whole. We just live in different houses.

I'm a single mum. I'll always be a single mum because I'm responsible for my sons, whether I'm living with Joe or not. It's a hell of a responsibility. It's not like looking after a cat for a weekend! Everything I ever do is for my sons. That's just my life, but I wouldn't have it any other way.

Lone parenting bears a stigma, probably not so much nowadays, but it was evident when I had Zach and was on my own. There's also an assumption that if you're with someone, like I am with Joe, you're no longer a lone parent. That's a really weird notion. I've done posts before about how proud I am of being a single parent, and people have written back saying, 'You're with Joe, you're not a single parent.'

As lovely as Joe is, as wonderful and as great a part of my sons' lives as he is, they are still my responsibility and always will be. It's up to me to make sure they're fed, clothed and have a roof over their heads. The buck stops with me. In my eyes, that doesn't change if I have a relationship with somebody, so I'll always wear the single-parent badge and I'm super-proud of it, never embarrassed.

Zach and Leighton see their dads every other weekend, and they have the time of their lives. They're spoilt rotten, and rules go out of the window. I understand that: it's the weekend and they haven't seen their dad for two weeks. When they're with me, I'm the one who says, 'You're not eating that', or 'You have to go to bed now', or 'You've got homework to do'. Sometimes I feel like the bad cop, but I wouldn't swap our situations because I wouldn't want to be a weekend mum. Their dads deserve to have the best time with them, because they don't see as much of them as I do.

I know that my children are deeply loved. I know that in the past we had a warped view about lone parenting, but that's changing, as is, hopefully, the notion that any unconventional family set-up is potentially damaging, or wrong.

As long as children are loved, it doesn't matter whether they are in a blended family, with a lone parent, a unit made of friends, a single-sex home or any other permutation of family life.

It's ridiculous to suggest otherwise. For me, it's about ignoring those headlines that say what we're doing isn't right or creates criminals. It's about cherishing the people we have in our lives, and doing whatever we can to support and raise our children.

STAY POSITIVE

Don't be afraid to embrace your new set-up. See anyone new as a positive addition from the get-go. No one else has the right to tell you your situation is wrong. There *is* no right or wrong. Trust yourself and your decisions. Shower your children with love and affection. Don't beat yourself up if you're having a difficult time and are banging your head against a brick wall: everyone's been there.

Remember that the notion of family can extend outwards from blood relations to the amazing people in your life. If parts of your family are missing, create new ones with friends who love you.

Let's celebrate the amazing work we do as parents, guardians, grandparents or carers in bringing up the next generation the best way we know how – with love, whatever it looks like.

CHAPTER 16

Thankful

Zach: '*Muuuum.*'

Me: 'Yes, Zach, what is it?' We were walking home one day when Zach was still at mainstream school.

Zach: 'So-and-so's got a new PlayStation. They're so rich.'

Me: 'We're wealthy, just in different ways.'

Zach: 'Yeah, that's good, but I want a PS4.'

Gratitude.

For a ten-year-old boy, it's pretty simple: being thankful for new technology so he can play games with his friends. Except that, ultimately, stuff doesn't matter, and people do. I don't give my boys a lot because I don't want them to feel too comfortable, that everything's there on a plate for them. They assume everyone else is rich because they get everything and I say, 'No, we can't buy that game. We can't afford it. It's thirty pounds, too much.' Whenever Zach asks for the latest gadget, I say to him that we're rich in love because that, for me, is the greatest gift I've ever received: the love of my family. I'm working on being thankful with them every day.

I'm always grateful. Sometimes I worry that I'm too grateful because it can diminish my right to be where I am in life. I probably need to balance my gratitude: I'm gushing, 'Thank you so much for letting me have this job,' and forgetting to recognize that perhaps I got it on merit!

Joe and I are really similar like that. In our industry, most people are thinking, I've been asked because I'm fantastic, and that level of confidence must be amazing to possess. In contrast, Joe and I can't stop thanking anyone who gives us a job because neither of us was born to this kind of life, and there's a big part of us that still can't believe we're on telly. It's not that we don't realize we're good enough, it's just that there are so many people out there who are good enough, and we're privileged in having the opportunities we're given. I'm so grateful that *Loose Women* asked me to be a Loose Woman. They hadn't had anyone like me before so I can imagine it was quite a tough decision to have someone who was younger, with less life experience, someone completely new for their audience. It was a risk for the show, but it really paid off. I recognize that I do a great job and I work really hard, so I'm not putting myself down when I say I'm overly grateful, but I also know that others out there are just as deserving.

I'm really grateful to *The X Factor* for what it did for me, and the doors that opened as a result, though people say I worked hard and stuck with it. I know lots of people who have exceptional voices and great personalities: they would be phenomenal on that show, and they haven't been offered the opportunity. Of course, that makes me wildly grateful – there'd be something wrong with me if I wasn't. There's always someone out there who has the same talents but isn't getting the same breaks.

In my experience, I think women are more grateful than men when they're given good jobs or career breaks. When we're 'allowed' to do it, we're so thankful, while men will say, 'Hire me, I'm amazing.' Gender may make a difference, but for me it was circumstance.

The way I grew up, and the circles I was mixing in, meant that I never dreamt I would be doing what I'm doing now. My circumstances meant that was never a reality. Even though I dreamt of being a singer, in the back of my mind I was convinced it would never happen, and that makes me thankful too. It was totally outside my experience, and that of the people around me. It was such an impossible, faraway dream. I still get days when I think to myself, *Oh, my gosh, how did this happen?!*

I'm overwhelmed by how I got here.

Being thankful is so much easier for me because I didn't grow up feeling success was owed to me. I didn't feel I was deserving of it, not because I wasn't good enough but because I didn't imagine that was the life set out for me. I didn't think it was my path. Growing up in Dagenham isn't a sure-fire route to stardom! When, all of a sudden, my dreams were within reach, then coming true, it instilled in me a desire never to take anything for granted, to appreciate every single second, because it could disappear as quickly as it came.

I'm always checking with my sons on their ability to be thankful. They're incredible kids, though of course I'm biased! They'll volunteer with my step-mum and work with elderly people. They see how difficult life can be as you get older. I try to make a conscious effort to show them how lucky we are. I remind them every day that we have our health, we have each other, and that's everything. If they have a meltdown when I say no to a new piece of technology, I ask them: 'Where's your head at? You're so lucky already. You have so much, you don't need any more.'

When we go to events, there are always gifts or goody bags with toys, and if I can't give mine away, I'll hide it for Christmas or a birthday. I struggle with giving my children stuff for no reason. Either they must have achieved something, or they've done something really kind, or it's a birthday. Otherwise how do they learn the value of anything? And if they don't know the value of anything, how can they be thankful for the things they have? I don't necessarily mean the monetary value, though that's important too: I mean the value in how they feel when they've achieved something or worked really hard. I was brought up with a strong work ethic. Both my parents worked long hours and made sure we never wanted for anything. I want my sons to reflect that ideology too.

Together we discuss why things can be unfair, while drawing comparisons with our own lives. It might sound a bit harsh but I want to foster empathy in my children. We are surrounded by people struggling with different challenges in life and I want the boys to appreciate that. It comes up all the time in real life. We can be walking down a street, and one of the boys will say, 'What's wrong with that girl?' or 'Is that boy okay?' I explain to them that they may have an illness or a disability, and may be struggling with things my boys cannot comprehend. It's about counting our blessings and how that makes us more sensitive to what others may be going through, while enhancing our ability to enjoy life.

If I took each day for granted, I'd miss appreciating everything this life has to offer, even its stresses and hardships.

I had two babies – wow! It blows my mind because there was only a short biological window when I was able to conceive. When I had Zach I didn't really know how, when and why I got pregnant. I wasn't having sex that often. I was a young girl experimenting with my sexuality. It happened that I did it on a day when a sperm managed to swim up my fallopian tube and fertilize an egg. So much has to go right for that to happen.

There are so many miracles around us. Gratitude gives me that kind of perspective. I look out at the garden and see trees and plants growing, and I think, Wow! This just happens and that's amazing! How do plants communicate with each other? How do they know which leaves to evolve to make sure they get enough sunlight? How do the bees know about pollinating flowers? How did I end up here with this tree and that bee?

Then I look at people. I might see someone on the train and I'll focus on them, asking myself why they're on that journey. How come we're on this train at the same time, going in the same direction? I've watched people help someone across the road, or I see someone struggling with a pram on the tube: another passenger appears from nowhere and helps them. The human race is blimmin' fantastic! I'm thankful to be a part of it.

Every day I try my best to make gratitude a conscious state of mind because it makes me happier. When people say, 'Thank you' to me, and I can tell they really mean it, it makes the world a better place. Practising gratitude, perhaps by writing a daily list of things to be thankful for, is so important. We have so much to be grateful for: clean air to breathe, a fairly politically stable country, food on the supermarket shelves, sunshine on wintry days …

Today I can honestly say I'm truly grateful for:

My health – being alive, being able to walk around and use my body.

My family – I couldn't imagine my life without them.

My job, and everything I have in my life as a result. There's not one bit of my life that I wish wasn't there, and that, in itself, is something to be grateful for.

My boys and their ability to live at top speed, entirely in the moment.

The support I've been shown time and time again by my friends, family and followers. What an amazing lot you all are!

Being able to write this book and connect with you guys out there. I love you all!

I find that my mindset is completely different when I'm consciously thankful for every experience that comes my way, even the bad ones, because it's always a chance to review, start again or find the silver lining when the cloud seems more black than grey.

STAY POSITIVE

Writing a gratitude list can even help to improve symptoms of mild depression. It's a powerful exercise, and can transform how we feel about our lives in just a few minutes each day.

Write a list of everything you feel thankful for in your life. It can be small things or big, life-changing things. This is especially important when you're feeling down, because the simple act of being thankful can help you refocus on what's good and what you have that perhaps you're not appreciating. Once you're thinking about things to be grateful for, it becomes easier to start noticing things to appreciate and turns into a positive, happy spiral upwards. Gratitude breeds gratitude. It just gets bigger. Be grateful for the uncomfortable stuff, too, because everything we experience is teaching us more about ourselves and the world around us.

CHAPTER 17

My Happy Ever After

'Race you to your flat! It'll be hilarious!' I shouted, the wine I'd been drinking all evening sloshing around in my system. I was pretty drunk. All my first-date nerves were replaced by giddiness.

'Are you sure that's wise, Stace? I live on the fifth floor,' Joe answered, staring at me like I was a total buffoon. He'd barely drunk any of the bottle I'd brought with me for our first official date.

'Course it is! Bet I'll beat ya!' I don't know what possessed me. I rarely, if ever, drank alcohol, yet my friends had told me to have a few drinks to calm my anxiety over my first night in with Joe. He'd invited me to his place to watch movies and eat dinner. It was the first time I'd ever been there, and I was nervous at the thought of sitting with him.

'Does he think I'm going to have sex with him?' I'd asked my girlfriends. 'What if he wants to and I don't? If he wants dinner, why aren't we going out to a restaurant? What if I come across as a right weirdo?'

My friends said, 'Have a glass of wine, take the edge off it,' because that would make me less nervous. Obvious, right? So, I had a drink with them before I left. I turned up at his house with a bottle of wine, because apparently that's what people do. I'd never turned up at someone's house with a bottle before but I thought, If the worst comes to the worst, I can just drink the wine and forget about the whole thing.

I got round there, found the glasses cupboard and poured some wine. He didn't appear to drink his. I don't like the taste of wine but I gulped it down – bad idea!

We ate and I carried on drinking this red wine, and then it ran out. I remember Joe saying: 'Has it run out already? Have you drunk it all?'

I replied indignantly, 'No, no, I've been pouring you glasses,' but really his glass had remained full all that time. 'We should get some more.'

'You want some more? Okay, I can take you to the shop,' Joe said. Honestly, I think that's the only time he has ever seen me drunk. We went down to the shops, and when we came back, I said, 'I bet I beat you if I run up the stairs.'

Joe was like, 'No way!', so I got all competitive about it. 'I bet I would!' There I was, challenging a man I hardly knew to a race.

Who cared if I was quicker than the lift? What on earth was I thinking? I was trying to make a good impression because I really fancied him.

Joe jumped in the lift while I legged it up the stairs. Minutes later, I arrived at the top. I was hyperventilating.

'I beat ya! I told you I would …' I started to feel really ill.
Joe opened the door to his spotless white bachelor pad.

'Oh, my gosh, I'm going to be sick!' I saw a look of panic
on Joe's face but the room started to go all weird, and
suddenly I had no control over the vast amounts of red
wine pouring out of my mouth all over Joe's white walls
and floors.

I tried to focus my eyes and saw red blotches all over the
floor.

'Oh, my God, are you okay?' Bless Joe, he was more
concerned for me than for his lovely apartment. It was
probably the most embarrassing moment of my life.

Because I'm a massive hypochondriac, I was wailing: 'I
need an ambulance. I need my stomach pumped. I'm
going to die!'

By this time, my head was drooped over the toilet bowl
and Joe was kneeling next to me, saying, 'You're not going
to die, Stace, I promise.'

'I want to go home,' I cried.

'Just stay here. You can't go home like this. Do you want
me to stroke your head?' Joe asked.

We were in for a long night. I wouldn't let him go to
bed, so I made him sit up all night in case I passed out,
inhaled my sick and died. Seriously, how did I ever get a
second date with him? Later, Joe told me he'd thought I
was acting really strangely and that I liked getting drunk!

The next day I can't tell you how humiliated I felt. I had
the worst headache and could barely open my eyes. I just
wanted the floor to swallow me. He was there, and all I

could think was, Get away from me. I couldn't bear him seeing me in that state.

He kept asking if I was all right, and I pretended I was. I wanted to teleport myself home so I didn't have to have a conversation with him.

'But what about your walls?' I whimpered.

'It's only paint, innit?' Joe laughed. He was completely unbothered.

All I can think is that he must have liked me to go out with me again.

Apparently, Joe and I first met when I was crowned Queen of the Jungle on *I'm a Celebrity…* but I don't remember, it was all such a whirlwind. We met again on *Virtually Famous*, where we were in competition with each other. We had a giggle, and a bit of a flirt. I thought he was really attractive and kind-hearted but I wasn't interested in having a relationship. I had shut myself off from that kind of attraction. I was thinking, I don't have time. I've got two kids, a dog, a huge mortgage to pay. I've got stuff coming out of my ears. I wasn't in the right frame of mind.

He pursued me, though, and his persistence in taking me out and meeting me after work was attractive. He started growing on me. It didn't make him feel knocked-back that I said no: it made him want to take me out even more.

Then when I went out to Australia to do the panel on *I'm a Celebrity…* we spent a week together, and when I left, he came up to my hotel room to say goodbye, which I thought was really sweet. I said, 'Goodbye, see you later,' and shut the door. I carried on packing. There was another knock at the door, and he just walked into the room and planted a big kiss on my face, which was really awkward. He finished, said goodbye again and left. I didn't speak to him for twenty-four hours because I was on the flight home to England.

After we'd got back from Australia, he came and met my family. He was so brave, turning up at mine for Friday-night dinner and being bombarded by fifteen or so of my relatives. We'd been talking to each other, and seeing each other casually, and I think me saying no to a relationship made him even keener. When I allowed myself to start to get to know him, I discovered how funny and lovely he is, and that he doesn't realize how attractive he is. I saw that he walks into a room and effortlessly makes people laugh. He's endearing. He's got time for people. He's got so much compassion – he really cares about you even if he doesn't know you. The way he speaks about his son is very attrac-tive – he puts in lots of effort to have as great a relation-ship with him as he can. Putting family first is high on my list of priorities when it comes to building a relationship.

Joe is also really smart. He has the same issues as I do with his accent, and almost believes he's not smart, because people tell him he isn't. He has lots of social and emotional intelligence. He's able to read a room. If you were upset, he'd go over and say, 'Are you all right?' with-out you even having to open your mouth.

He is also really practical. He has this puzzle brain, as I like to call it, and he can work stuff out. My brain works differently. If you tell me a formula I'll remember it and apply it. His works by figuring things out.

I never felt like we were falling in love in the spotlight. The way I look at it, Joe is not a massive superstar. He's one of those celebrities who has managed to stay grounded and normal. I genuinely felt I was falling in love with a normal person. It didn't feel like we were some showbiz couple. Once we'd 'come out' and made our relationship official, we were photographed together and people seemed so happy about it, telling us, 'You're so perfect together – you have to make this work. Don't lose each other.'

At the start it put a lot of pressure on us as we didn't know each other that well. It felt weird that our relationship might have an effect on other people. We're not Brad and Angelina! We're just Joe and Stace, and we're able to get on with it like a normal couple.

The press will always paint a picture of us as they see us, which perhaps isn't really as we are. Like the marriage rumours: everyone thinks it's me that's pushing for wedding bells, but I think Joe wants to get married more than I do. I like the idea of it, but it's another form of conditioning. Little girls grow up fantasizing about putting on a white dress and a veil, and apparently that's going to happen to me and I should want it.

I'm so used to questioning everything that I naturally bring that frame of mind to thoughts of a wedding. What would we gain as a couple? Is that the only way we can demonstrate our love for each other?

On a practical level, we're from different backgrounds: Joe isn't religious at all, and I'm Jewish, so we wouldn't be able to have a religious ceremony together. I don't see the sense in a wedding: let's be frank, it would cost a *lot* of money. I'd rather have our house together and more children, though we both like the idea of declaring our love for each other with all our family around us. We're trying for a baby. We've moved in together. So far, so good!

I believe Joe's 'the one'. I wouldn't think of procreating with him if I didn't believe that. I thought my previous partner was for ever, but things change, people change, and perhaps they don't want the same things any more. I would be naïve to think it could never happen again. I've been in a relationship that's broken down and I had no control over it. I've got to an age where I have to stop being 100 per cent trusting, especially when it can affect my children. For the first time in my life I've thought, I can look at the world with rose-tinted goggles, thinking it's all wonderful, but when it comes to decisions that affect Zach and Leighton, I have to be really savvy for their sake.

Relationships are complicated. Mine and Joe's works so well because we're really similar *and* really different (I know that sounds crazy). Our jobs are super-similar, so we understand what it's like to be in the industry we're in. It's very unstable. We never know where the next job's coming from. We don't know where we'll be from one day to the next, or what a job may lead to. It would be harder to communicate with someone who doesn't understand that dynamic. We work in the same industry but rarely together. He does his thing and I do mine. We both know how exciting and busy it can be at one minute, then quiet the next. You never know where your next pay cheque is coming from, not that I'm complaining: I think I have the best work in the world. We have that common ground. Joe knows if I'm worrying about something because he's most likely been through it himself.

Our backgrounds help us. Weirdly, and this freaks me out a bit, Joe is really like my dad. Their lives are almost a mirror image of each other's. Joe grew up in the same area as Dad. He lost his father at exactly the same age as Dad did. I would say aspects of their personalities come from losing a parent. I see the same drive in Joe as in my dad to provide for his family and be a great father.

From my experience of watching my dad be a parent, knowing that he lost his dad, I can see that he overcompensates. He is a part of every aspect of our lives: he doesn't want to miss a moment. He never wants us to feel as he did. Not only does he worry about not being around for us in a physical sense, he strives to be present, no matter what, on an emotional level. He's incredibly caring, fun and witty. He cherishes every second of family life, and that's what I see in Joe too. Joe's ultimate goal is to be the best father he can be, and he spends much of his time working out how he can make the people in his life happy. That's wildly attractive to me.

I'm sure both men would have been like that anyway, but it's accentuated by the losses they suffered. The passion Joe has for his family made me fall in love with him.

When it comes to politics, Joe and I are totally different. I'm such a leftie! Joe isn't right wing, but his views are different from mine so we have little arguments. Our tastes are different too. Joe loves in-depth history, murder or crime stories and scary films, while I love *Pretty Woman*, basically any rom-com, anything that's happy and light. Joe listens to blimmin' conspiracy theories on podcasts in bed, and scares the frickin' life out of me – I make him wear headphones.

Food is another thing. I eat *so* much. When we go for a meal, I know exactly what I want, but he dithers: 'Am I going to be jealous of what she's having? Should I order the same or get something different?' It drives me nuts. Then he orders something rubbish, which I would never want to eat, and insists we share.

I don't fuss about anything day-to-day, while Joe really stresses out. Every day during our house purchase he asked, 'Have you done this? Have you signed the paper-work?' while I was super-relaxed, knowing it'd all work out in the end. I kept having to tell my boyfriend to calm down. He's always convinced things will end in disaster.

I grew up on Disney, believing I was going to meet my Prince Charming and ride off into the sunset with him on a white horse. We would live happily ever after and that was that. When my parents got divorced, I accepted that story wasn't for everyone. But then I realized that fairy-tales come in different packages, and at different times, because Dad met someone else and fell in love. I learnt there are variants of the dream: there doesn't have to be the one take on it, the one Prince or Princess Charming. That felt like a huge relief, and helped me see relationships in a tentatively positive light.

Obviously when I got pregnant with a partner I knew wasn't my forever after, I saw that my Disney fantasy wasn't going to come true. I spent quite a long time assuming it wasn't for me because I became a single mum with two children by two different fathers. In a weird way, I almost felt I didn't *deserve* to find my Prince Charming – until I met Joe. Being with him has reminded me that I can have that dream of loving and being loved by someone. It had never gone away: it was just on pause for a while.

Being with Joe is amazing. He does so many things that melt my heart. Because I was working I couldn't make it to the last day of summer football camp to see my boys pick up their trophies. Later that day I got a text from Joe with a picture of him and my boys holding their trophies. I didn't ask Joe to go because I didn't want to put that pressure on him, but he knew it was the last day and said he'd go. When I got that photo of them, I cried with happiness, then wondered why I hadn't ask him to go in the first place. Perhaps there's still a part of me that can't quite believe this is happening, that this person loves me and I can lean on him.

Joe and I really love each other. As we've been together just a few years, I don't feel I can give advice about making relationships work, but what I can say is that the differences add to our relationship. The quirks broaden our knowledge and help us have more empathy towards each other and other people in our lives. In understanding him, and in loving him as a complete package, I've learnt to create a foundation of mutual respect and affection that we can build on. Our relationship feels solid. It feels like we can go the distance, and there's something magical in that calm, steady knowledge after the first few months of romance settle down into whatever the relationship will become.

Joe and I have loads of fun together – it's the best thing about our relationship. I'm no love guru, but I'd say we could all work at being kinder to each other and ourselves, and ramping up the silly times is never a waste.

Who knows what the future holds? Who knows if we'll still be together in five, ten or twenty years? What I do know, is that I love him, he's a buffoon, like me, and being together feels like my fairytale has come true.

CHAPTER 18

Musings on Imperfection

Perfect: *Having all the required or desirable elements, qualities, or characteristics; as good as it is possible to be. Free from any flaw or defect in condition or quality; faultless. Highly suitable for someone or something; exactly right.*

Oxford Living Dictionaries

Happiness has nothing to do with perfection: it has everything to do with love and connecting with the people and the world around me. Yet how many of us fall into the trap of thinking, If I just had that car, that partner, that house, I'd be happy?

When I was becoming aware of what society was telling me I needed to be happy, I really thought I had to become this perfect human being, with a perfect life, to exist happily. I didn't know it at the time, but stuff – money and material things – is as far away from what really makes people happy as you can possibly get.

Of course, we all like to treat ourselves now and then, it's human and enjoyable, but when it comes to lasting joy, then keeping up with the Joneses can be a sure-fire way to feel bad about yourself. We've all known someone who looked like they 'had it all'. Perhaps they were stunningly pretty and everyone wanted to go out with them. Perhaps they were talented or funny, and were the popular one at school. Perhaps they had a really cool dad who took them on special trips or bought them loads of trendy gear or up-to-date tech gadgets. Perhaps they could eat cake till the cows came home and never put on a pound, or had amazing holidays when our parents could only afford a soggy tent in Wales.

Whatever it was, there was something we wanted that they had.

What we didn't realize was that behind the perfect façade there was a real person with the same amount of difficulties or challenges as we had. It was just that they seemed so much better in every way that we didn't see it. Some of the most academic pupils are stressed. Some of the prettiest people feel ugly inside. Some of the children with loads of gadgets get them because their parent has to be away a lot for work. Behind every image of perfection there is real life.

We're all humans and we all make mistakes, make idiots of ourselves or fail at something. Seriously, we'd be robots if we didn't. Even though now, as a grown-up, I can see through it, while I was growing up I had a really clear idea of what would make me happy: becoming rich, meeting

Prince Charming and being swept off my feet. Obviously I'd also have a perfect home with 2.4 kids and a 4x4.

How wildly, unbelievably wrong I was.

The main thing I've learnt from looking at my own crazy ideas about what would bring me joy is that it was so far removed from my current imperfectly happy life. The reality of my happiness has nothing to do with the perfect constructs I dreamt of. As always, it's the small things that make me so happy – the fun times, the people I meet, the places I go – none of which I could have predicted.

The stuff that is totally imperfectly brilliant, that makes my life complete, is the things I already had. Looking back, as I wrote my list of what would make me happy, I realized that I had always had everything that makes me happy. A revelation! My family always were the source of my happiness, I just didn't know it at the time. Their love *is* my happy.

I don't have to look outside my tribe to find joy: it's already right there. I have a deep-rooted sense of belonging, and I'm lucky to have it. They give me so much, I can hardly put it into words: comfort and laughter, protection from the tough times, loving parents and siblings, a big extended family … When I gave birth to Zach I suddenly realized how important family was to me. I had this massive security blanket, people who looked after me and made sure I got through times, such as the fracturing of the relationship with Zach's dad, that would have been so much tougher without them.

I tell my boys every day how lucky they are to have such a fantastic family. I want them to understand how privileged they are! I want them to know that their happiness is not governed by how many Nintendo Switches they have, or how well they play Fortnite: it's all about people, the love they show you and the love we show them. We have to cherish love and return it to live our fullest, most satisfying life.

Experiencing the world is something I have discovered that makes me happy. I don't necessarily mean travelling to far-flung places, though that's wonderful. I enjoy going to villages and towns in the UK as well as different countries, and meeting new people. I enjoy learning everything I can about the planet I live on and the places I go. There is so much to discover, so much in science and nature that just blows my mind. We're so lucky to inhabit this planet in our solar system. What a miracle it is just to be born. If I'm waiting in a queue at the supermarket checkout, I try to remember what a privilege it is to be in that queue at all!

I love experiencing what the world has to offer. I'm a sociable person, and I love chatting to people, finding out about their lives and hearing their stories. I also love trying new things. The other day I booked myself into circus training. I wanted to try something new, and have fun while I discovered what amazing new things my body was capable of. I loved it! I'm always saying to my boys that they should have a go at that new class, or enrol in a new sport, so I thought it was time I took the plunge. I don't think I'll ever have a career in the circus but it was super-fun, and I laughed a lot.

Watching my children laugh and play, achieve or not-achieve fills me with happiness.

Everything to do with my boys makes me happy. Even if they're having a terrible time I never lose sight of that. When I first had Zach, I thought my life was over and I wondered if I'd made the right choice. I can categorically say that having him and Leighton were the best decisions I ever made. Becoming a parent is tough, but it's everything to me. The boys can be giggling together, or playing a game, then five minutes later they're falling out. Two minutes after that, they're making up shows to perform to me. They're a bundle of energy and joy, and I love the chaos and the fun! Saying that, I'm a worrier so I take my responsibilities to them very seriously. I vowed they would always have a roof over their heads, food in their tummies and the best life I could possibly give them, and I do everything in my power to make that happen. Now that Joe and I are living together, we've become a blended family (yay!). We'll be doing everything together as one family from now on, as well as trying for our own baby to complete our family. Sometimes I sit and watch Joe wrestling with the boys and feel overwhelming love for them all.

That's my happy. Every time.

Food is a big source of joy to me. Mealtimes make me happy because they're a chance for our family to get together, but food as such makes me really happy too. Weirdly, I've discovered that an extremely large proportion of the texts Joe and I send each other are about food.

In fact, I've noticed that often I don't bother replying with words: I just send him a photo of what I'm about to eat. Joe does the same.

My favourite comfort food is pie 'n' mash. I often text Joe a picture of my plate of pie, mash and gravy to show him that nothing comes before my dinner – not even him. Whenever I need some serious comfort, I go to a proper pie 'n' mash shop in Barkingside. If I'm there and he texts me to find out what I'm up to, I just send him a photo of my meal. I always text him photos of my famous roast dinners if he can't make it on Friday night. With that one image, I'm gloating: 'I've made a roast and you're not here!' I'll also send him photos of whatever I'm cooking, like Nana's meringues or yet another roast. I'm particularly proud of my Yorkshire puddings.

Joe makes me happy, though it's important to recognize that I was happy before I met him. He brings a whole new dimension of happiness to my life but I was very content without a partner. Often we think our fairytale has to involve somebody else, but it doesn't. He makes me extremely happy, but I can be happy without him. I think sometimes we can end up in the wrong relationship because we're worried that as single individuals we'll never have that happy ending. It just isn't true.

It's funny how we have all these goals when we're younger. When I get the big house, nice car, amazing career, gorgeous hunk and kids, I'll be happy, we think. Yet everything that makes me happy was there before I started looking: my family, my curiosity about the world, my love of food – all of it was part of me. All that's happened is I've built upon it so I now have more people to love, more interesting people to meet and places to go because of my job.

I put so much pressure on myself when I was younger – I have to get that, I have to go here. I believed I wanted so much more than I had. And I created a life similar to the one I grew up in. It was through having children that I realized what I value most in life is family and love. I learnt so much more about myself, and how I really love and appreciate my family. When we're younger, our parents get on our nerves, don't they? I used to think, *They don't know anything, they haven't got a clue about me*. When I had a child, I was like *They know everything!*

Everything they said was right!

Did your parents ever say to you, 'When you've got children of your own, you'll understand'? Well, I used to think, No, I won't. I won't be anything like you! I'll really get my children, I'll really understand them. When I had my own, I felt like saying, 'Mum and Dad, I'm so sorry!'

This is my happy ending right now, but I'd rather it was a happy infinity! I don't want anything to end – ever. My relationships with people are the best parts of my life, the most rewarding and fulfilling aspects of my existence. The material stuff didn't make the cut when I took a long, hard look at the things that bring me the most joy. There will always be good and bad parts of our life. Hardships and sorrows are inevitable – but so are the good times, the fun and laughter.

If, like me, you can recall what you thought would make you happy as a child, why not write a list of everything you expected or wanted? Dig deep and look at the expectations you had growing up, or the things you thought you should want, regardless of whether they actually fitted you, your personality and life. It can be incredibly revealing to put the spotlight on all those forgotten dreams or fantasies. I found it funny but also quite one-dimensional.

I noticed that much of what was on my list was what society expected of me, or was a form of conditioning I'd received from the world at large. It bore very little resemblance to anything that might genuinely make me feel good. Sure, it'd be great to have millions in the bank but we all know that money, in itself, can't make us happy.

This is a list of the shoulda, woulda, couldas – and it's interesting how they lose their power by being brought out from the recesses of your mind into the light. Looking at mine made me realize how far I've come from those fantasies, and how much richer and more amazing my life is as a result. You could compare your list to how your life actually turned out. I bet it's way better – and way more chaotic, funny and challenging.

STAY POSITIVE

None of us is perfect. We're all ridiculous in one way or another. Let's celebrate that by enjoying each and every one of our flaws, the bits we get wrong, the parts of us that are so-so. Like me, you might want to write your list of everything that makes you happy, ignoring the things you tell yourself to strive for.

The differences might surprise you. It's a game-changer.

You could take a journal and write a Good Experiences Guide to your life. The list could stretch for pages, detailing every laugh-out-loud moment with your family, every spine-tingling kiss or shared embrace. It could include every shared glance, every stifled giggle, every moment of pure peace or beauty. Experiences make us who we are. Remembering the good ones, the incredible ones and the earth-shattering ones can be uplifting.

That's where the love and the light are.

CHAPTER 19

Forget the 'How-tos'

've always hated being told what to do.

As a child, I rebelled at school. My mother despaired and worried endlessly at how I'd turn out – but I turned out okay, I hope. Let's face it, most of us will never be rich, famous, twenty-one again, breathtakingly beautiful, married to a Russian billionaire, or invited round to the Beckhams' house for a glass of wine and low-carb nibbles. So, all the How-tos – you know, the messages we get everywhere, daily, telling us How to Get Beach Body Ready! How to Attract Your Soulmate! How to Get Rich By Doing Nothing! How to Be a Perfect Mum/Wife/Daughter/Dad/Husband/Son are all absolute rubbish.

It can be hard fighting back against all this pressure.

I've found that the more I like myself, the more I understand how counter-productive it is to body-shame or hate myself. Liking myself becomes really enjoyable – it actually becomes a bit addictive. When I like who I am, I'm loads less worried about things that mean nothing, and I spend more time telling myself nice things than horrible ones. I feel better. Because I feel better, I think I look better. In a way, I'm better as a person because I'm being kinder to myself.

If I feel beautiful, no one can take that away from me. I'm trying not to buy into the marketing industry any more. When I'm about to buy something, I ask myself, 'Do I really need this moisturizer?' Most of the time, I don't. I just like the packaging, or the photos of beautiful models who advertise it, and there's nothing wrong with that. I don't need to buy new clothes for every single occasion: I can wear the same thing twice, and who cares if people judge me? I don't need to wash my hair with mega-expensive shampoo or line my bathroom cabinet with hundreds of pounds' worth of goop. It saves me a lot of money when I find I'm absolutely fine without it all.

That doesn't mean I won't get my nails painted, or I won't put on make-up or spend money on new clothes, but I do it a lot less often now that I'm much more accepting of myself. I'm really comfortable in my own skin, and I think it's because I started asking myself, 'What is all this marketing about?' and 'Why am I chasing this impossible goal? Where's it going to get me?'

I have lots of close friends who have had surgery to correct a part of their bodies that made them feel down. I've noticed that afterwards they'll move on to something else that upsets them about themselves. I have no judgement about plastic surgery. Do it, if it makes you feel good. Don't do it if, like me, you're not sure it would make your life better. But it's true that every time we try to tweak one bit of ourselves to near perfection, something else jumps out at us. It's a never-ending drama. Sometimes I'll notice that my eyelashes don't look long so I put on fake ones. Then I'll think, Oh, my lips look too small, so I put on extra lip-liner. By then I'm thinking, Is there ever such a thing as perfect? Is it even possible, or are we just programmed to want more? Also, is the image of perfect always going to be something that isn't me?

I don't feel I'm ever represented in the world of fashion or beauty, in any kind of advertising. They always use one type of person, and there's only ever going to be a minority of humans who look like that, so the rest of us just carry on trying to fit in, buying whatever they're selling us, because we don't.

Isn't that the point, though? You have to buy the stuff to stand a chance of looking 'right'.

I have to bat off the How-tos. I have to put up a defence against them: it's so easy to get bogged down with How to … wean your baby, How to … pick the perfect partner, How to … have the best relationships with your friends, How to … reconcile with your partner, How to … be a good parent, How to … look the best, How to … be the skinniest or, even, How to … live!

It's everywhere.

Everyone is trying to give us information about how to be something else, or how to achieve something in life. I feel so privileged to have lived in the time of the internet. I can't imagine how anyone found out anything before it existed. Yet wherever we go, whatever we're doing, somebody is trying to tell us how to do it better.

It's on advertising billboards, online blogs, vlogs and websites, social media, telly, in magazines and newspapers. I have to skip past it on my newsfeed, and not take it in if I happen to read it because otherwise I'd go crazy. I don't need to be bombarded with any more information telling me how to be better at being alive.

It's difficult, because everyone lives intricate, complex lives, so the how-tos will only work for a few people, not the majority. I totally accept the need to have information and I get why we need guidance and advice. The stuff that isn't helpful for me is the drive for perfection. It can knock self-esteem, and make us wobble on the paths that we thought we were doing okay on.

Despite that, those moments when we're shaken and start questioning ourselves can be really positive: they make us look at new ways of behaving or being. Questioning ourselves can also be detrimental, if it means we question our abilities or strengths. I believe that self-analysis needs to be selective: I find it's about using my own instincts and intuition to discover what helps me live my best life, and what really doesn't. It's about making a choice to seek that information.

In my work for *Loose Women*, I meet people who have kicked back against the how-tos because they've fought stigma or prejudice. I'm always inspired by the human-interest stories I cover, like when I had the chance to meet Baroness Lawrence of Clarendon, OBE, Stephen Lawrence's mother. She lost her teenage son to knife crime, went on to campaign for reform within the police service, and set up the Stephen Lawrence Charitable Trust. People like her go through grief, trauma and devastation yet still manage to change the world for the better.

If being told nasty things online makes me feel bad, I imagine what it's like to face the prejudice and the hate that Lady Lawrence and her family went through, even from the police, whom we're supposed to trust and rely on. She didn't conform to the way in which we expect people to react in those circumstances. She didn't get angry. She didn't throw the hate back, but did the most incredible, loving, strong thing and changed the world for her community. There are no how-tos for growing up in poverty, dealing with injustice and the grief that comes from that. How-tos have generally sprung from the myriad responsibilities we all have.

Being an adult is not a burden, but it's challenging and testing. When I'm making decisions for myself, I know that any outcome is uncertain, and I feel I can be responsible, seek out relevant information if I need to, then deal with any consequences of that decision, and it'll be all right. When it comes to my boys, the stakes are higher when I don't know the outcome of my choices. I hope everything will be fine, and they'll grow up being happy, balanced individuals, but there's always that uncertainty.

Acting like an adult is also a bit of a struggle for me because my inner child keeps popping out. When my kids are teasing each other in the back of my car, screaming with laughter when one of them farts, that's when I pretend to be a grown-up by telling them to shush because Mummy is driving. What I really want to do is sit in the middle seat between them and laugh. When Joe is playing a computer game with me, I laugh so much at how rubbish he is that he ends up getting angry. All I can think is, I'm such a child. Why didn't I stop winding him up?

My siblings and I used to terrorize Mum when she was driving us to see Grandma. We'd sing songs too loudly, muck about and, if we were lucky enough to stop for a MaccyD's on the way, we'd blow bits of paper across the table using our straws. We wound her up something chronic. It was childish but it made us happy.

These days, I don't know when to tap out of my inner idiot. At big telly meetings I have to tell myself, 'Stace, you're at work, you're in a serious environment, you're not the class clown any more' … except, of course, I still am. I have to bite my lip to stop myself cracking jokes. That's possibly when I need to read the How to Be Professional blogs, or How to Act Like a Grown-up At Work. We have to have the confidence to follow our own codes, to take in what makes us better and stronger, and discard the rest. Not easy.

Filtering through masses of information, selecting what is a good fit and throwing out what undermines us is hugely challenging – and time-consuming.

I don't miss the freedom of just having me to worry about. On the contrary, I don't know where I'd have wandered to just having responsibility for myself. The boys gave me focus and determination: there was always a reason why I was getting up and going to work, fighting to be a success for them. Without them I would probably have been quite complacent, bobbing along and perhaps not achieving much.

My philosophy is always to value myself, the people in my life, and our 'normality'. I have learnt to disregard most of what is thrown at me across the media. It's so important for my quality of life. We all have days when we're more vulnerable to the how-tos, when we're tired, stressed-out or angry, but as long as I keep remembering that I'm okay and no one is going to convince me otherwise, I can laugh off those messages. In fact, I'd say ignoring the how-tos most of the time is essential to feeling okay about myself: I get to rely on my instincts and my sense of what's real or not.

My counterbalance to the how-tos is pretty cringy, but it's always about learning to love myself, to accept all my frailties and failures, my how-not-tos, basically.

By snuggling up to my mistakes and the wonky parts of my personality, I gain freedom from the pressures that beset most of us from all angles. When I'm happy with my how-not-tos, I can ignore or question the reams of advice and opinion out there. It takes practice, and most of us won't fall in love with ourselves overnight. For many of us, it can be a lifelong journey to achieve even self-acceptance. We have to try.

It's the only way we can refocus our gaze away from the how-tos and really appreciate that we're okay as we are, and don't need to be told how to achieve anything. I'm not saying I fully love and accept myself. I have days when I wobble, when I question myself and my abilities, but over time they're becoming fewer because I work hard on enjoying my life and loving who I am. I know I like being in control, which I don't really love, and I know that some days I can be socially awkward.

When I was introduced recently to a *Loose Women* director I've known for years, instead of being relaxed and acknowledging we knew each other, I was fumbling over my words. I said something weird and formal to her, then had to backtrack. By now, everyone in the room was feeling uncomfortable, but I carried on, trying to wave it off, not very successfully.

What an idiot! Why couldn't I just say, 'Hi, nice to see you'? Even worse, I wouldn't let it go and continued, talking too loudly, while the director was probably thinking, What's wrong with this girl? I find that funny now, though at the time it was excruciating. Learning to love my quirks doesn't mean they vanish. It just means I'm okay with them, and I'm not hiding parts of myself from others.

STAY POSITIVE

Self-love and self-acceptance are the keys to hitting back at the how-tos. If you can step away from your mistakes (we all make them) and see them for what they are, the state of being human, you're coming from a much more emotionally healthy place.

Be nice to yourself. Talk yourself up, appreciate your strengths, and tolerate your weaknesses with a kind of resigned humour. Lighten up and the world lights with you. Don't compare yourselves to others: that way madness lies.

CHAPTER 20

Kindness

Seeing the good in everyone isn't always easy, is it? Yet being kind is probably the single most effective way to keep the world turning than anything else.

First and foremost, I'm kind for selfish reasons.

I like how I feel when I'm helping someone, and I don't like how I feel when I'm being horrible. I just don't cope well with people being upset. I've noticed that I get a different reaction from others if I'm nice to them. It's so simple but really effective.

My glass-half-full mentality tells me that most people are good at heart, most people want to be nice to others, so it would be unfair of me not to reciprocate.

It's vital to my wellbeing that I'm good to those around me. I don't want to make anyone miserable and I would find it harder to like myself if I treated people unfairly. I think that goes for all of us, but sometimes little hurts can escalate into big ones and before we know it we're fighting with our spouse or yelling at our children. It's so easy to lose our cool, these days, though I don't think we should put on a hair shirt and beat ourselves up over it because that's counterproductive.

I believe that most people are not unkind on purpose. I think they act in ways that may not be beneficial because they're perhaps under pressure at home or at work, or from other issues in their lives. If I'm a bit moody or snappy, I know something is going on to make me behave like that (raging hormones mostly …) so I figure it must be the same for everyone else. There will be a reason behind bad or unkind behaviour: knowing that, I can be more compassionate and sympathetic. I don't think I've ever met anybody I thought was born mean, bad to the bone or just pure evil. Most people are a product of their circumstances, and emotions are easily triggered by what's going on in their lives – so much so that it's a wonder we're all as civilized as we are!

I guess it's about recognizing that we all have bad days, days when we get defensive or cross with others. Being nasty for the sake of it is not the norm – I don't care what anybody says. My family and friends tell me I'm hopelessly naïve yet they're the same underneath. My dad would help anyone in need, as would any member of my family. They wouldn't need to be asked twice, and I think, deep down, we're all built this way. I have absolute faith in humanity's goodness, and when I act like I believe that, others show me they can be trusted.

Kindness comes in many different forms. Sometimes it looks like being tough with someone. That doesn't mean it isn't kindness: it can be a form of tough love to help someone move forward with their life. My friends were sometimes very straight with me, especially when it came to dealing with pregnancy – they really helped me keep my feet on the ground when sometimes I felt the world was collapsing around me. Tough love, they call it, and I realized it was for my own good and their way of showing they cared. If I assume people are doing things for the right reasons, I'll be nicer to them and, hopefully, they'll be nice to me. If I embrace the possibility that people are kind, it generally works out that they are.

I've had so many acts of kindness shown to me through my life, and it's not only the grand gestures I remember. On my first day at secondary school I was sitting on my own until someone came to sit next to me. That gave me a great feeling of relief and happiness. Everyone was scared. No one knew who their friends were going to be, what lessons we were going to do, where the toilets were … Terrifying.

That day in the lunch hall, it happened again. I remember a girl called Stacey. She had red hair and I thought she was really beautiful. I was sitting alone at the table when she just sat down beside me, saying, 'I heard we have the same name! I'm called Stacey as well!' We'd all had our names called in Assembly and she'd remembered – it made my day.

It's so often the little things that are memorable and feel important. For example, I'm really bad at remembering new people's names but Joe's brilliant at it and he will make a point of saying names out loud to remind me if I join a conversation with a group of people at a party or event. That always strikes me as really kind. It doesn't have to be something huge like raising enormous sums of money for charity, or walking across a desert for a good cause. It can be something as simple as looking out for each other and compensating for a loved ones shortcomings!

Little things mean so much.

My dad's the most openly kind person in my family. He has no boundaries. If he was walking down the street and saw someone with heavy shopping bags he'd ask, 'Where are you going?' then take the bags and carry them to that person's home. I can't tell you how many times we've been on the way to somewhere in the car and he's pulled over to help a stranded motorist change a tyre, or tow them, or jump-start them.

We were always late as kids because of my dad's inability to ignore someone in distress. I got a real sense of it being the right thing to do. It was different from doing a favour. Dad doesn't give to receive: he just does it, without thinking. He taught me to 'Do unto others as you would have them do unto you'. It's a brilliant philosophy.

If I help somebody, I hope I won't ever need any help, but if I do, I would hope there'd be somebody around to help me.

Of course, it's not always reciprocated, but I'd say nine times out of ten it is. There aren't many occasions when you see a car broken down and someone hasn't stopped to help.

There'll also be times when you have to drive past – you'll be late to pick up the kids if you stop or whatever it is – and that's okay as well. We're not superhuman. Sometimes we have to step back and let others help because we're not in a position to do so. It's an act of self-kindness, of self-care. Just having the awareness, hoping the person who's stuck is okay, can be enough.

If I felt I was doing something that upset people, or going about some matter in the wrong way, it would eat away at me and I would question my intention. Sometimes we get stuck and dwell on negative things. Therapy is good at unlocking these feelings and helping you accept that you might put a foot wrong sometimes, but that revisiting it again and again will not help. Rather, we need to be able to move on. Counselling can be so useful in helping us shift our perceptions when we're out of sync with our own values and inherent goodness.

I volunteer at the Soup Kitchen, a homeless shelter on Tottenham Court Road. I love my time there. I mostly serve the tea and coffee, but the other day I brought in Bingo because I thought we could all play together. Sometimes I'll make stuff to take, like Rice Krispie cakes, but a lot of the time I'll just chat and have a laugh with the people the charity helps. I'm interested in how they ended up there.

From the outside, someone might say I'm the one helping or being kind, but that's not true. Those people help me by letting me into their lives, telling me their stories and helping me to evaluate how grateful I am for all the good things in my life. From the outside looking in, you'd probably think they have nothing, but the kindness and laughter I experience when I'm with them just blows me away, and it's why I say that being kind can be selfish. I come away uplifted by the human spirit. People endure shocking lives, poverty-stricken backgrounds and the worst injuries, illnesses and losses you can imagine, yet I'm greeted with smiles and treated to entertaining conversation and that special ingredient, hope, every time I go there.

There's one lady who I can talk to for ages. She lost her husband, her child, and her way in life, yet she's happy. She's homeless. She lives on the street not far from the shelter, yet she laughs all the time. She teaches me to appreciate the simple stuff, like a cup of hot tea on a cold day, or a burst of sunshine after rain. She tells brilliant jokes and makes us all laugh. Her spirit is unquenched by the adversity she's suffered, and I admire her for that.

I really enjoy being around people, and if I have a few moments to spare, why not try to be around people who need interaction, conversation and hot food? Again, it's a selfish act. It brings me so much satisfaction that it can't help but be selfish. I feel really good about being involved, so I take every opportunity I'm given to do some charity work. My agent constantly reminds me that I have no time, but I always say, 'Who knows what's round the corner? It could happen to us one day!'

Small acts of kindness can have big consequences. On social media, writing back to someone, or clicking the 'like' button, can make their day. There's so much power in interacting kindly. Obviously, I can't reply to everyone, but I try hard every day to reply to as many people as I can. I love having conversations with people I've never met, and I like them feeling that I care.

Without people commenting and taking an interest in the things I do, I wouldn't have the career I have, and I wouldn't be a part of social media. I feel I have a responsibility to my followers, and I like showing I appreciate their support. I wouldn't be able to do my job without it. I like to let people know I'm not leaving my social media in the hands of someone else to build a business. It's me replying, not a PR team putting up pictures – I wouldn't see the point in having a social media account if it was. People interact with me, and delve into a side of my life that I'm willing to share, and vice versa. There is a lot of unkindness online, and on social media. It makes it doubly important we relate to our followers in a human way, and reach out to people with the best of intentions.

So many small acts of kindness light up my days, but my favourite is being sent a text by someone I haven't spoken to in ages or sending one to them. Making that connection and showing whoever it is that I'm thinking of them, or discovering they're thinking of me, is amazing. I love it when the boys or Joe wash out the bath after they've used it so that when I want to get in it's nice and clean. That's seriously thoughtful in my book! Asking someone if they're all right can feel good too, and I love it when people do that for me if they haven't heard from me in a while. I really appreciate it if someone notices I'm a bit sad or less than my usual jolly self. It can make all the difference to how I feel.

Topping up the water in the fridge. Another biggie for me. At home, we don't drink bottled water so I put a jug of tap water in the fridge. You can imagine how I feel when I go to get a drink and find someone's finished it and put the empty jug back. When they do remember, I'm so happy to find cold water for me. Wa-hoo!

Saying thank you, even if it's ages after the thing you're grateful for, is always nice. I love the look on my family's face when I thank them unexpectedly, and I really like acknowledging that people have helped me in some way or given me an opportunity. I love saying thank you.

Giving away old stuff can feel satisfying. When I moved in with Joe, I gathered up sackfuls of clothes, toys, random things from the house, and gave it all to charity. De-cluttering *and* helping others. Amazing!

Remembering to be kind to *yourself*, as well as to the people around you, is so important. Try writing a list of all the amazing qualities you possess. It might feel a bit strange at first so start with two or three things that are great about you, and go from there.

This follows on from the idea of being able to love and accept yourself. Building up a list of all the things you feel are good, worthy, or plain fabulous about yourself is a nice boost. It could be as simple as you make a great cup of tea, or you're a brilliant listener, or you're kind to someone who really frustrates you. Maybe you've been a good friend to someone, or you picked up the phone when someone needed a sympathetic ear, or you did a small but significant favour to somebody you barely knew. Whatever it was, from making soup for an ill friend to picking up a child's toy in the street and returning it, from minuscule to large, write down everything that makes you a good, decent person. Once you start, I promise it becomes easier.

When you have the list, which you can keep adding to as you remember things, pin it up for at least a week somewhere prominent at home. It's your visible reminder of how great you are, and that you should be kind to yourself as well as others.

We could all inject more kindness into our lives. Obviously, there are some people it's difficult to be kind to. Perhaps they've been nasty to us in the past. In that case, we can feel sorry for them, and think kind thoughts about them without letting our barriers down too much. If I don't feel I can be kind to a particular person, I just walk away. Better to say nothing than to be unkind.

Small acts of kindness can make my day a million times better. Doing something nice for others can change my mood, help me feel more connected to them and appreciate the good in everyone, including myself. Whether you're nice to people in person or on social media, it makes the world a better place for all of us.

STAY POSITIVE

Paying it forward. When someone's in need, whether they're a stranger or a friend, pay forward all the love and care you've received in the past by giving back. It might be calling someone and really listening to what's wrong. It's a privilege for someone to share their problems with you, or ask for advice. Listening is such a powerful way of connecting, and we've all had at least one experience of someone listening to us. Paying it forward is sharing the love, giving back and keeping it going.

Find new ways to express kindness. Write a surprise note, telling your partner or child how much you love them, and sneak it into their pocket or lunch box. There are so many ways to be kind that involve very little effort yet reap huge rewards.

CHAPTER 21

Happily Imperfect Habits

E very day when I wake up, I can choose how I feel. That doesn't mean there aren't stressful things happening in my life, which I may be worried or sad about, it just means I can look at how I react to whatever is going on. It's the only real control I ever have over anything.

If I react negatively to someone saying something I don't like or to a situation I feel I don't deserve, I'm at the mercy of that person or situation. I can form happily imperfect habits that free me from the need to react in a way that doesn't serve me. That doesn't mean I'm a saint. Far from it! It's about allowing myself to choose. I try to step back and think, How am I going to act here? or What does this mean to me? or Is this really that important?

My happily imperfect habits have carried me through so much. I had to form them in my schooldays when I was the class freak. They helped me to make the best of my situation and not take things too personally. I'm sharing what I learnt about coping with sticking out like a sore thumb. We really are worth it. I am enough, and so are you. You're amazing, inspiring and incredible just as you are.

My biggest happiness habit is smiling. Easy, right? Smile – even if you've got giant teeth!

That's already kind of happily imperfect! I love my smile, and I love smiling. I feel that it makes a massive difference to how I feel. For some reason, those muscle movements in my face make me happy. Sometimes I get home in the evening and my face hurts because I've smiled so much. When I smile at someone, they almost always smile back. I bloomin' love it!

That's the best habit ever. Singing helped me smile a lot. If you don't want to be flat on the note, smiling helps you hit it. My singing coach Yvie Burnett taught me that. Maybe smiling makes everything sound and feel nicer. If I had the hump, you could tell from the position of my mouth. You'd know if I was happy or angry from my face. Your expression, a frown or a smile, dictates the tone of your voice, the way you react, and how people react to you. When I'm smiling, I'm happily imperfect.

Learning to love my flaws turned around my whole way of thinking about myself. Loving everything about myself felt really weird and hard, but when I did it, I discovered there was nothing wrong with me. It was really liberating. I stopped looking at myself as something or someone to fix. Instead, I just got on with my day, wore what I wanted to wear, did my make-up (or not) and got out there doing the things I loved. I'm happy with my imperfections, because I don't believe they're imperfections!

Embracing positivity was the game-changer for me. When you're feeling upbeat, nurture it. Store it in your emotions bank. Feed the positive thoughts. Concentrate on liking yourself and thinking the best of others. There are times, of course, when chemical imbalances or difficult events make it easier to be negative, and that's totally understandable. We shouldn't embrace positivity to the point where we deny real feelings that need to be processed. I think of it more as an inner glow, as a way of being, but it doesn't undermine the feelings we all need to experience. Store some positivity for those times when things get really challenging. We only have to look at the world around us to see that people are going through horrors and traumas. It is hard to be positive when faced with that, day in, day out.

I try to think of all the caring and nice people who do loving things every day to balance out the negative news onslaught. That way, I can acknowledge what's going on without trying to change it, or getting depressed about it. I can still keep my focus on the good things that people do and experience.

We all have positives in our life, as well as negatives. Now I make a conscious effort to soak up the majority of positive things that come my way, and take my focus off the negatives. It's tricky at first, but it's like training a new muscle: after a while, thinking positively becomes second nature. I can help flag up injustices or challenges people are facing through the work I do on *Loose Women*. I've been inspired so many times by how people have risen above their circumstances, dealt with unimaginable loss, and come out the other side, often as crusaders for justice or truth.

Thinking positively is harder than being cynical or pessimistic. It takes courage to look on the bright side. If I'm falling into negative thinking, I talk to Joe or a member of my family, and very soon I'm laughing again, or they'll reassure me that 'It'll all be fine', and it usually is.

Sharing what you have with those you love is a brilliant happy habit. There's no point in having anything if you've got no one to enjoy it with. My family and friends are mostly in the same circumstances they've always been in so we always do low-cost stuff together, but I'll always chip in and help wherever I can. I don't want to do stuff on my own: I want to do it alongside my family and the people I love.

Sharing isn't just about money or things, it's also about sharing problems, listening to friends and family, and being listened to in return. I share my thoughts, feelings, emotions and difficulties with the people around me, including my friends on *Loose Women*. We know each other's lives so well, and that's the thing I love the most about my job: being able to share my colleagues' troubles and experiences as I share mine.

Sharing fun, laughter, tears and problems makes me happier because I feel connected to the people I love. I love being there for them. I love it when a friend confides in me, or asks for my advice. Sharing the challenging as well as the good times is how we know we have real friends or caring family. Share more. Share everything – most especially, yourself.

Receiving love sounds obvious but how many of us are rubbish at being looked after or cared for? I know I can be because I want people to think I'm independent and a strong woman. Strength comes in loving, and being loved. The latter is just as important. It's about letting ourselves be loved, and feeling good enough for that love. Even if life is a series of stops and starts, and things haven't gone the way you planned, we are all worthy of being loved.

Being able to receive and accept that we're entitled to love and affection is a skill. For quite some time I imagined that a life of real love wasn't really for me, and then I met Joe. Things might not have worked out the first time, or the second, and it can be difficult to open up again to receiving love. Perhaps we fear our dream of being loved is selfish or unattainable. Perhaps we're scared of opening up to another person. It can be hard to trust someone when they say they love you. Take a risk. Open up – and see what comes back to you.

Let your light shine in its own true-to-yourself way. Be bright. Be unapologetic about it. That's a great habit to learn. We all know there's nothing worse than dimming your light for someone else. There have been times in my life when I've been afraid to be who I am because I didn't want to make anyone feel uncomfortable or embarrass myself. Then I thought, No one has the right to stand in the way of my light! I decided to shine as brightly as I could, doing the things I wanted to do, and people could decide if they wanted to be with me or not. Otherwise I'd have felt suppressed. The inability to be who you are is oppressive. It's not good for the soul. If you're being who you really are, it makes it easier for other people to be themselves. It gives them permission to shine too. We are all a work in progress but remember that you are good enough.

Do whatever it takes to become yourself. Be the best version of yourself that you can possibly be. Be clear about what you want, and who you are. Accept your weaknesses and work with your strengths. Get whatever help you need to do this, from a friend, business partner, counsellor or mentor. Remember that failure is just a way of learning more about yourself. It helps to grow a thicker skin, but if you show your true light, you'll attract your tribe, the people who shine in the same way.

Seeing life as an adventure is the habit I love most because it opens up normal things into wonders. No one really knows what's going to happen – ever! You can have it all planned out but you don't know what's around the corner, what new experiences you may have or new people you may meet. What could be more adventurous than that?

We think we know, but we don't. To me, that means I can put things down to experience. I can always try again, even if I fail a million times.

Self-love is a habit we all need to cultivate. Self-acceptance is surely the only sane way to respond to life on our incredible planet. Be nice to yourself – you're awesome in your own unique way. You will have much more time to appreciate, be grateful for and love all of the things that are happening around you if you already love yourself. Self-love is described in the dictionary as 'regard for one's own wellbeing and happiness'. This can come from eating well, exercising, sleeping eight hours, seeing true friends, spending time with your partner, being silly with your children and so on. There are so many individual ways to nurture your love for yourself, yet so many of us just don't have the time – or think we don't. Take time to do the things that increase your sense of self-worth. Love yourself – and the rest will follow.

It all comes back to being thankful. Count your blessings daily, if not hourly. Say thank you. *Feel* thanks. Just by being alive, we have reason to be grateful.

STAY POSITIVE

The good news is that habits can be learnt. Try out a few new ways of relating to yourself and others. Don't be frightened to think outside the box, to shake things up a bit and experiment with who you are and how you think and feel.

CHAPTER 22

Being Happy

feel like a fraud.

I feel like I've had a super-privileged life. I've had my ups and downs, as we all do, but I haven't suffered trauma, there's been no big challenge to get over, so it's been easier for me to find my own joy. When I was small, we were really hard up, but I didn't have a clue. I didn't know what we didn't have, I just knew I was happy. We didn't have a comfortable living, but I had no idea until I was older that my parents struggled financially. We had a home. We had food on the table. We were so loved and felt so safe and secure that the material stuff was irrelevant. I know that society says money is a privilege, but to me, the real privileges are your circumstances, your family and friends, the people who love you.

Yeah, my parents broke up, but they made it so painless and smooth that afterwards we were a better, bigger family.

Yeah, I got pregnant really young, people judged me and I struggled at the time, but I had my family as my safety net.

Yeah, I deal with unkind comments on social media and in the press, but I don't let them destroy me because I have so much love directly around me.

Anything I've ever had to deal with, I've been scooped up and taken through it by lots of people who were – are – there for me. That has made all the difference. It has turned things from disaster to a bump in the road. Many people out there are dealing with things alone, and have no one to help and support them. I have so much admiration and respect for those who have to hold their lives and emotions together on their own. It's a courageous way to live. As much as I might be praised for my positive mental attitude, it's actually come about because I'm surrounded by people who think in the same way. I don't think I'm especially resilient, I've just been lucky enough to have loads of love and support through everything I've faced, and it's rubbed off on me. I have never been left to cope alone.

Ultimately, it's up to us to work through things and learn how to be happy, but without people guiding us, that can be deeply challenging. At seventeen, I didn't know what to do when I found out I was pregnant. I had to get through that experience myself, but I had the help, guidance and advice of my family. Without it, my recovery from post-natal depression after Zachary's birth may have been much slower, my decisions less sure.

Happy is my default emotion. It's my neutral state. Even when something not so nice is going on, I generally think, Oh, well, and that's how I cope. We all cope differently.

My sister Jemma gets stressed more easily than I do, and there's nothing wrong with that: it's how she is. We're all wonderfully, wildly different.

I'd much rather go with the flow, be happy and not worry too much. To get stressed, upset or angry about something takes a lot of energy from me. Because I fear the ultimate, nothing really gets me going, or makes me feel on edge. When people ask me, 'Stace, what's your ten-year plan?' I have *no* idea how to answer, because I don't have one. I don't like thinking that far ahead. I just want to live now, be now, feel now. It makes me impulsive. If I see a last-minute deal online for a flight, I'll book it without thinking: living entirely in the present has its negative side – it can be quite dangerous for my bank account. This way of thinking can also be helpful: I don't worry about things that may be looming in the immediate future. I tend to block out everything that isn't happening today.

I live mostly in the moment. It drives Jemma crazy because she's always planning ahead: she likes to know what she's doing and when, and often she has to remind me of what's coming up, or organize me because she knows my head is solely in the experiences of the day.

Life is scary. None of us really knows why we're here. All we can ever do is find out what makes us tick, what gives purpose and meaning to our lives, and live by the values we cherish. My sister's happy to be stressed. She likes being on top of things, and that's her happy. She can cope with life much better when she's thinking of the future and occupying her mind here, there and everywhere. Someone outside looking in might think, She's so stressed, or She worries too much, but that's *her* happy. When Jemma's running around sorting stuff, her mind doesn't get the chance to wander. She doesn't get fazed by the big questions of life, such as 'Why are we here?' or 'What's the point of being alive?' or even 'Who am I?' She's too busy and, because of that, she can live her best life.

I'm pretty rubbish at saying no and I want to do everything that's asked of me. It means I get to support loads of fantastic charities. So being a bit overworked, time-short and busy is actually my best, happiest place because I feel I'm making a small difference to someone's life.

Knowing who I am, and liking who I am, is my happy. It makes me feel comfortable. I accept all the strange things about me, all my worries, because there's always a positive side. It makes me feel stable and happy just knowing that, because I'm mentally able to turn things around if I need to.

Finding our happy doesn't mean we're going to walk around with a smile on our face all the time, it just means we find our most comfortable way of being. We get to discover *our* happy – and that's going to be different for each person because we're all unique.

To deal with the meaning of life, I look at my world, live in my sphere and enjoy what I've created. The rest is out of my hands. It's not about being super-human, it's about liking who I am and recognizing I'm only human. That gives me peace, and a sense of accomplishment at the end of each day, however small.

When you're not consumed with what you look like, what you sound like, how you dress or who you are, you can just 'be'. You can enjoy the moments as they happen. When I'm happy being imperfect, and accepting who I am, warts and all, I find I have so much more energy to do the things I care about. I accept I have no control over other people, which leaves me free to look at my own life.

I'm not happy all the time. I can be unreasonable, snappy and moody, just like anyone else. Recently, I was sitting filling out forms for Joe's and my mortgage. They were really important. They were concerned with what happens if our relationship breaks down, or if one of us dies, the stuff I don't like dealing with because I have to imagine those scenarios. While I was doing it, Joe was sitting next to me, making a tapping noise on his phone. He might as well have been playing a snare drum. I ended up shouting: 'Will you shut up? I'm trying to write about something really important.'

Usually I wouldn't have noticed the noise.

I kept going: 'You've got no consideration for what I'm doing here. You don't even care!' I was totally overreacting, probably because filling out the form had triggered in me a feeling of fear about the future. In the end Joe went and had a bath, leaving me to it. I can be a stroppy cow just like anyone else!

The key to my upbeat nature must be that I'm no good at grudges. You know how some people remember for years when an argument broke out and why it upset them? Well, I always forget, sometimes within minutes of it happening. In the heat of the moment I might be upset but I can almost guarantee that a couple of hours later I'll have completely forgotten about it.

It comes from my parents never allowing my brothers and sisters to hold on to a quarrel. So, if I stole Jemma's clothes, they'd tell me off and tell Jemma to drop it, that it was finished. We weren't allowed to carry on an argument, and if we did, we'd get into trouble. Even if I was *so* right, and they were *so* wrong, it just wasn't allowed. Having years of my dad telling me to 'Drop it' and 'If you can't get over it, it's your issue,' made me rubbish at remembering when someone was horrible to me.

I'm pretty forgiving. Even if someone has done something silly or hurtful towards me, I can't believe they've done it on purpose. Again, it's naivety, but a positive part of it. I know how to forgive people so I don't carry resentments for years. I always think that when someone's nasty, it's more about what they may be going through.

I feel so much gratitude for all the good things in my life, and that makes me happy. I appreciate what I have rather than worrying about what I haven't. I don't compare myself to others. Instead, I concentrate on trying to be the best mum, best daughter, best girlfriend, best co-presenter and best friend I can be. I don't want to bring anyone down. I want everyone around me to feel as happy as I do.

I'm so glad to be alive. I enjoy feeling happy, and having my glass half full. I take the Shallow Hal approach to life, and sometimes it's a bit ridiculous. Once someone smashed my car window, took my keys and my purse but left the car. I drove to Ford to get a replacement window, then rang Mum and said: 'You know what? I've got a nice breeze coming through my window.'

Mum said, 'Stacey, someone just robbed you …'

My reply was: 'Well, yeah, I suppose so, but just think about the person who robbed me …'

'How can you right now, Stace?' Mum said, after a brief pause.

Me to Mum: 'Whoever robbed me must've really needed that money. To go up to a car, smash the window and possibly hurt themselves, get arrested and end up in jail to get twenty quid out of my purse because they know I'll cancel my cards, how desperate must they be to do that?'

Mum: silence.

This is such an unpopular viewpoint on *Loose Women*. People tell me I'm naïve and ridiculous, and I know it sounds like I'm making excuses for criminals but I'm so glad I don't feel I have to smash car windows for money. Anyone who's happy and comfortable in their life wouldn't take that risk. So I felt sorry for whoever had robbed me.

People will say to me, 'What about criminals who don't have to steal but do it anyway?' Well, that's even sadder. I don't condemn someone outright until I know the context they grew up in.

Hard times are part of life, I don't deny it. When I look at them as teaching me how to create a positive from a negative, I can think, It isn't perfect, but how could this be better? How can I make better choices? Who am I in this situation, and what are my values? I find then that challenges become opportunities.

I may be only twenty-nine but I've been lucky enough to live several lives: as a single mummy, a singer, a telly personality and chat-show host. I've loved and lost, made mistakes, and come out smiling. I live an imperfect life and I'm so grateful for that. I don't know what my 'perfect' would look like, but I do know that in keeping a sense of childhood magic alive, in finding the joy and fun in normal everyday living, I've been able to pick myself up countless times, brush myself off and plant a smile back on my face.

I love my life. I love every second of it. From wondering if I'd ever amount to anything, to being catapulted to fame, all with the love of my family, it's been a journey, and I hope I can pass on any help I've been given in sharing my experiences with you. I'm paying it forward in the hope that the things I've learnt will be as useful to you as they have been to me. A lot of the time, my life feels hilarious. When I'm clearing up cat sick, or scraping Nutella off the kitchen table while emailing my agent about a trip to LA, or chatting to journalists about a promo, I sometimes look at myself and laugh. It's all so blimmin' bonkers and brilliant.

If I could impart some good old-fashioned Essex wisdom, I'd probably start with the fact that smiling beats frowning every time – and I'm pretty sure it gives you fewer lines. Assume that everyone you meet is inherently kind, unless proven otherwise. It takes away all the effort involved in working out someone's motives or thinking. Assume positive intent, and I guarantee you'll make yourself happier because you won't always be worrying if someone means what they say, or if there's an underlying agenda. Thinking like this makes my life so much easier.

At all times, be more like the lady I love from the homeless shelter I help out at. Imagine being that happy, and having nothing. We could all do with being a bit more like her, I reckon. Tell your children, partner, family and besties you love them *every day*, because you never know what's round the next corner, and while you're at it, forgive and forget – life is too short to hold on to grudges.

Never give up your dreams. Your circumstances don't have to determine how you'll do in life, unless you let them. Most of the time, things aren't as bad as they seem. When you hit a hole in the road, it doesn't mean you can't fill it with tarmac and drive straight over it!

My favourite bit of advice would be: when opportunity comes knocking, say a resounding 'Yes!' Say yes, think later. I feel it's better to say yes and not achieve something, rather than say no, and not try. At least in trying something new, there's a possibility that something exciting may happen. If I'd been told that queuing up for hours to sing at *The X Factor* trials would bring me to where I am now, with wonderful followers, a career on telly and so many amazing new things to experience, I wouldn't have believed it. Yet it's all happened – and I'm so grateful for every moment of it.

I think we should all be more Peter Pan. If you've ever watched the film *Hook*, you'll know the scene where they go for dinner and there's nothing in the bowls. Peter Pan has to use his imagination to envisage the food. All of a sudden, he goes back to his childhood self and he sees steaming piles of food yet the bowls are still empty.

Try to live your life like Peter Pan because everything looks better from a child's perspective. Use your imagination to make experiences in your life shine.

Learning who you are is the most important part of your education – and that doesn't necessarily mean you learn it at school. When I was younger I always wanted to be Rachel from *Friends* – she had the coolest hair, the prettiest face and then the fashion designer career – but in reality I was Phoebe, the weird one. Nowadays, I love being a Phoebe. My weirdness is one of my biggest assets!

Know that we are all enough, however, whatever and whomever we are. Love who you are, because then it's easier for other people to love you. Love everything about yourself – the wobbly bits, the quirks, the lop-sided boobs, ears or eyebrows.

Make a conscious effort to tell yourself that you're amazing. You're an incredible, resourceful human who is capable of so much. What's not to love?

Happiness isn't a choice for those people who suffer clinical depression or other mental-health problems, and I'm so grateful I don't have to deal with that kind of illness. That's why it's even more important for me to choose happiness, because I *can*. I'm one of the lucky ones. I can whack on a smile and look for the silver linings. I'll always be the girl who gets excited about fake nails or sitting in pig poo!

So much about being happy is about choosing to see the positives. It's about cultivating resilience in the face of reasons to be miserable, and that's how we keep growing as a person, through the not-so-easy times as well as the good moments.

When I'm faced with a sad news story, a friend getting hurt or one of my children being upset, I try not to get worked up because that seems to increase whatever negative feelings are being expressed. Instead, I try to take an emotional step back and look at the situation with a little perspective.

I have a few sure-fire ways that help to swing me back into a happy place, even when I'm confronted with sadness. I like getting together a bag of stuff for the charity shop. Somehow it makes me feel I'm doing *something*. I call a friend I haven't spoken to for ages, and enjoy the connection with someone in my life. I take the boys for a walk, possibly to talk things through or just to have an adventure. Being outside, breathing in the fresh air and feeling the sun or wind on my face helps my mood shift up again.

They're such simple things, and I'm sure there are a million others you could try to reset your happy dial.

Next time you're faced with a situation that might baffle or upset you take a chance. Try choosing positivity even when every cell in your brain is firing off negative thoughts. Take the positive road and appreciate just how far you've already come. Every day you wake up, you're winning. It's as simple as that. Why not choose happiness?

Stick up for yourself and others – where I come from, it's important to have each other's backs. Gather your allies. Say your truth. It's the Dagenham way.

Last, treat others as you wish to be treated, and don't ever give in order to receive.

You're going to be fine.

STAY POSITIVE

We're all humans, trying to live our best lives. Loneliness and isolation are the scourges of our time. They shouldn't exist. If you know anyone who might be slipping off your radar, or who may need a friendly call or chat, it's time to reach out to them. If it's you who is feeling lost or alone, then perhaps it's time to gather your courage, pick up the phone and tell someone. Help and connection may be closer than you think. You may even be helping someone else by leaning on them.

It may be worth writing down who your friends and loved ones are, and how you feel close to them, through shared humour, taste in music or silly jokes. Reminding yourself that you're part of an interconnected planet with a living, breathing human race may tip you out of loneliness and back into where you belong. We have a birthright to feel loved and to love in return – it's what makes us humans rather than robots. Exercise that right as often and as warmly as you dare and see how your connections open up and expand.

Epilogue

Thank you so much for buying my book. I really mean that. Honestly, it's such a privilege to be sitting here with you while you read these pages, a cuppa in one hand, probably, and maybe a Digestive in the other (am I right?). I hope I've made sense, and shared a few bits about how I live my life in the best way I can.

No one's life is perfect. Not even celebrities have ideal worlds. We're all just weird, wonderful human beings, and thank goodness we are. If we can all remember that, and be a little kinder to each other, I reckon we'll be all right.

If there's anything I've learnt it's that whatever I'm told by the media, by advertising or society, it's that I'm already enough. No face pack, no plastic surgery, no perfect home will ever make me feel complete. It just won't. It's a myth – but there's nothing wrong with treating myself and living the best life I can for me and my sons.

I am *so* happily imperfect. Happiness comes to me in so many different ways: in Zach and Leighton's smiles, in mucking about with Joe, in a phone call with Jemma, in eating Turkish food with Dad and Karen, or enjoying time with the rest of my incredible family. So many rays of happy imperfection fill my days.

I know I'm privileged to feel as I do. I also know that I've had some dark days, and I've been through a lot, but I've learnt that there is always a silver lining no matter how black the cloud, and often the silver is spell-bindingly beautiful. I love my life in all its weirdness and silliness. I honestly wouldn't have it any other way.

It's about being a grown-up too – carrying my responsibilities but always keeping a smile on my face or a cheesy joke to hand. Like you know you're an adult when you ask Santa for a Hoover for Christmas. Well, I'm definitely a proper grown-up these days, and I have two happy, healthy, fun-loving boys to prove it. I dedicate this book to them.

Love you,

Stacey xxx

PS And if all else fails – A Recipe That Says, 'It's All Going To Be Okay, Even Though We're All Going to The Same Place in the End, And No One Has Ever Been Declared Immortal – Yet.'

Great-Grandma's Meringues

At any moment of crisis, indecision, or when we're all just needing a sugar hit, I make these for Joe and the boys. It's usually when I'm having a dark-night-of-the-soul moment, worrying about my mortality, that this recipe for happiness provides metaphorical relief. They're amazing, though no one has ever perfected them like Grandma did. Her meringues were an art form: perfectly crunchy on the outside and chewy in the middle. It makes my mouth water just thinking of them. Now that she has passed away, I love making them even more, because I feel connected to her when I'm whisking away, covered with icing sugar. They're a fitting tribute to her, and this is her no-fail recipe for about 20 small meringues. To make these beauties, you'll need:

3 large egg whites
200g icing sugar, sifted

Preheat the oven to 140°C/Gas 1.

Whisk the egg whites in a clean bowl until you have stiff peaks. Add the icing sugar slowly, a tablespoon at a time, whisking until the meringue mixture is nice and glossy.

Line a baking tray with baking paper. Spoon meringue into a piping bag and cut the end off. Pipe the mixture onto the tray in little blobs, making roughly 20 small meringues.

Put them into the oven for 1–1½ hours. You'll know when they're ready as they'll be a bit golden on the outside and will peel off the baking paper.

Acknowledgements

I'd first like to thank the team at HarperCollins, especially Carolyn Thorne who gave me the chance to write this book. Thank you to Cathryn Kemp, who was there to help me put down the words floating around in my head day and night. Thank you for our long chats and the many laughs we had along the way.

I couldn't do any of this without my management team – special thanks to Angharad Marsh, Tom Wright and Stephanie Walton.

Love and thanks to my wonderful family, Mummy Solomon, Daddy Solomon, Jemma, Matthew and Joshy Solomon – I love you all.

Thanks too to Sam Sam Stone, Aaron Hewitt and Ray Hewitt.

And a special mention to Joe Joe, Shana and Cassie.